# NATION OF COWARDS

# NATION

## OF
### Black Activism in Barack Obama's
### Post-Racial America

# COWARDS

DAVID H. IKARD AND MARTELL LEE TEASLEY

INDIANA UNIVERSITY PRESS

*Bloomington & Indianapolis*

This book is a publication of

Indiana University Press
601 North Morton Street
Bloomington, Indiana
47404-3797 USA

iupress.indiana.edu

Telephone orders   800-842-6796
Fax orders         812-855-7931

∞ The paper used in this publication
meets the minimum requirements of the
American National Standard for
Information Sciences—Permanence of
Paper for Printed Library Materials,
ANSI Z39.48-1992.

Manufactured in the
United States of America

Library of Congress
Cataloging-in-Publication Data

Ikard, David [date]
  Nation of cowards : black activism in
Barack Obama's post-racial America /
David Ikard and Martell Teasley.
    p. cm. — (Blacks in the diaspora)
  Includes bibliographical references and
index.
  ISBN 978-0-253-00628-8 (cloth : alk.
paper) — ISBN 978-0-253-00701-8 (eb)
  1. African Americans—Politics and
government—21st century. 2. African
Americans—Social conditions—21st
century. 3. African Americans—Eco-
nomic conditions—21st century. 4.
Obama, Barack—Relations with African
Americans. 5. United States—Race
relations—Political aspects 6. United
States—Politics and government—2009-
7. Post-racialism—United States. 8. Race
awareness—United States. I. Teasley,
Martell L. II. Title.
  E185.86.I39                    2012
  305.8'009730905—dc23  2012017797


1  2  3  4  5    17  16  15  14  13  12

# CONTENTS

## ACKNOWLEDGMENTS

If it takes a village to raise a child, it certainly takes a village to write a book. Therefore, we'd like to acknowledge the family, friends, and colleagues who have been instrumental in helping us to write this book. I, David Ikard, would like to give special thanks to Anouchcka Ambouroue for putting up with me throughout this grueling ordeal. You are an angel. I'd also like to thank my colleagues Rhea Lathan, "Tayo" and Joy Onifade, Alisha Gaines, Maxine Montgomery, Wanda Costen, La Vinia Jennings, Mark Anthony Neal, Tracy Sharpley-Whiting, Richard Mizelle, William Jelani Cobb, Wizdom Powell, Lisa Thompson, and Monica Coleman. Whether you know it or not, you challenge me to think more critically, work more diligently and dream more ambitiously. Lastly, I would like to thank my beautiful children, Elijah and Octavia. You both inspire me to be a better scholar, parent, and overall human being. I am blessed to be your father.

I, Martell Teasley, am truly grateful and in debt to members of the Diop Institute for Scholarly Advancement for their challenging intellectual discourse and commitment to scholar activism. I am particularly thankful for my colleagues Reiland Rabaka and Zizwe Poe who have expanded my intellectual horizon with each conversation. My biggest and most important support system is, of course, my family. A heartfelt thanks goes to my wife, Tanya, my daughters Aura and Taylor, and our pet dog, Buddy. Without your love, patience, and sacrifice I could never have completed this project. To my son Martell; love, prosperity, and blessings—stay strong like the hammer but bend like the reed. To my daughters Marquita and Tiara, you bring great joy into my life and I am always thinking of you both; your success and promise to the world means so much to me. To my granddaughter Skye, you make our family's future bright.

# NATION OF COWARDS

# Introduction

## Is America a Nation of Cowards or Has Attorney General Eric Holder Lost His Mind?

In my previous writings . . . I called for the framing of issues in a way designed to appeal to broad segments of the population. Key to this framing, I argued, would be an emphasis on policies that would directly benefit all groups, not just people of color. My thinking was that, given American views about poverty and race, a color-blind agenda would be the most realistic way to generate the broad political support that would be necessary to enact the required legislation. I no longer hold this view.

The question is not whether the policy should be race neutral or universal; the question is whether the policy is framed to facilitate a frank discussion of the problems that ought to be addressed and to generate broad political support to alleviate them. So now my position has changed: In framing public policy, we should not shy away from an explicit discussion of the specific issues of race and poverty; on the contrary, we should highlight them in our attempt to convince the nation that these problems should be seriously confronted and that there is an urgent need to address them. These issues of race and poverty should be framed in such a way that not only is a sense of the fairness and justice of combating inequality generated, but also people are made aware that our country would be better off if these problems were seriously addressed and eradicated.

—*William Julius Wilson*

Though this nation has proudly thought of itself as an ethnic melting pot, in things racial we have always been and continue to be, in too many ways, essentially a nation of cowards.

—*Eric Holder*

1

IT JUST SO HAPPENED that we heard the media commentary surrounding Attorney General Eric Holder's now (in)famous "race speech" before we actually got the chance to hear the speech itself. The first black attorney general in U.S. history, Holder used his position as the nation's top law enforcement officer as a bully pulpit to warn Americans that racism is still alive and well in the nation. The mainstream media and blogosphere fixated on the excerpt from the 2009 speech in which Holder characterizes American as "a nation of cowards" on the issue of race. The mounting attacks against Holder—the bulk of which were coming from a mostly white and politically diverse group spanning from GOP celebrity Rush Limbaugh to liberal *New York Times* columnist Maureen Dowd[1]—created the impression that Holder was speaking out of anger and cynicism. The unfolding white narrative in the dominant media cast Holder in the role of the prototypical "angry black man"—a term used to describe a racially embittered black man who displaces self-imposed socioeconomic failings onto whites. More specifically, Holder's detractors argued he was ignoring the significance of Barack Obama's historic election as the first African American president as well as his own historic appointment as the first African American attorney general. Surely, white racial cowards would not have elected a black man to the highest and most powerful post in the country—if not the world—and supported another as the nation's chief law enforcement officer. With only a few notable exceptions within conservative black political circles, the African American side of the debate was unfolding in a radically different way. In the eyes of most, Holder was not an angry black man with a bone to pick with white folks. Rather, he was a brave and insightful black leader speaking truth to power. Whether they admitted it or not, whites continued to enjoy race privilege at the direct socioeconomic expense of African Americans and other non-white ethnic minorities. Holder was being attacked because he dared to hold whites accountable. In the black narrative, Holder emerged as a heroic figure, offering a salty dose of racial "straight-talk" to balance out Obama's lofty "hope" rhetoric.

When we reviewed the speech in its entirety for ourselves, we found both perspectives to be lacking in certain respects. On the black side of the debate, most commentators emphasized the lasting socioeconomic impact of slavery and Jim Crow to black self-determination as if Holder's speech was aimed exclusively at condemning whites. Even as Holder was undoubtedly trying to illuminate the link between white oppression and black self-determination, he was hardly giving African Americans a free pass on culpability. He makes clear in his speech that racial cowardice cuts across race lines. He also makes clear that when it comes to having uneasy conversations about race and racial progress in this country, the tendency for both blacks and whites is to retreat into established and overworn political postures:

> Our history has demonstrated that the vast majority of Americans are uncomfortable with, and would like to not have to deal with, racial matters and that is why those, black and white, elected or self-appointed, who promise relief in easy, quick solutions, no matter how divisive, are embraced. We are then free to retreat to our race protected cocoons where much is comfortable and where progress is not really made. (sec 1)

Even though Holder attests that, on a socioeconomic level, blacks have clearly suffered more in this country than whites because of slavery, Jim Crow segregation, and institutionalized racism, he demonstrates that blacks too have an inability to talk frankly, openly, and critically about race. He explains that our nation's stalled racial dialogue is not a white, black, or brown problem, but an American problem that has a disproportionately crippling effect on African Americans and other historically oppressed groups because of disparate power dynamics. To the post-racial and mostly white argument that Obama's election to president and Holder's appointment to attorney general demonstrate the rapidly decreasing relevance of race in the United States, Holder writes that persistent socioeconomic inequalities belie the notion that we live in a post-racial society. He underscores his argument by pointing out that outside of the workplace, America remains a largely segregated society. He opines, "On Saturdays and Sundays America in the year 2009 does not, in some ways, differ significantly [in interracial interactions] from the [segregated] country that existed some fifty years ago" (sec 3). What this voluntary segregation outside the workplace demonstrates for Holder is that there are still many social barriers on the issue of race left to overcome, barriers that are rarely engaged or scrutinized because our race rhetoric tends to conflate tolerating racial difference with appreciating it.

What we found rather telling about the diverging racial responses to Holder's speech is that most folks retreated to established racial postures in exactly the ways that Holder warns against. In the public domain, and the media in particular, Holder's complex argument about race was recalibrated or "dumbed down" to an us-versus-them/oppressed-versus-oppressor discourse. Depending on how an individual positioned herself in this manufactured dichotomy, she was either a racist or a victim of racism; Holder was either an insightful and heroic black leader or an angry black man with a racial chip on his shoulder. Lost in this polarized debate was a crucial point Holder was making in his speech about the radically changing racial make-up of our country. Holder reports that in a few decades we will no longer be a majority white nation even as the socioeconomic power will remain largely in the hands of whites. He views this trend as potentially dangerous because we have yet to productively reconcile the racial divide in America. He projects that if we continue on this path, we not only risk unnecessary and costly interracial conflict but also leave open the door to an apartheid mentality toward non-white groups in general and African Americans in particular. To emphasize his point, Holder uses the analogy of a rich suburban community that employs electronic padlocks to shield itself from the poverty-driven urban crime lurking outside its boundaries. He asserts, "It is not safe for this nation to assume that the unaddressed social problems in the poorest parts of this country can be isolated and will not ultimately affect the larger society" (sec 5). He argues that as a nation we are only as strong socially and economically as our weakest constitutive parts. If white Americans with wealth and power ignore the concerns of African Americans and historically oppressed groups, they directly jeopardize their socioeconomic stability. The socioeconomic health of black America has—and continues to be—a barometer of our country's socioeconomic health and well being. When African Americans thrive socially and economically then we are all better off.

Holder's thinking on this score bears a strikingly resemblance to the business philosophy that professional sports leagues employ to remain economically competitive and prosperous. Consider how the National Football League (NFL) and National Basketball Association (NBA) respond to their least competitive teams. Typically the teams with the worst records are given priority in the draft at the end of the season. The rationale is that by strengthening the weaker teams and making them more competitive, the league as a whole becomes stronger and more competitive. If, say, the Los Angeles Lakers and the New England Patriots were able because of their franchises' wealth to sign the best players year in and year out and, as a result, win the championships in their respected leagues every season, the NBA and NFL would eventually fold. And, of course, the Lakers and Patriots would fold as well because their value as franchises is tied to the league's overall financial success.

Tellingly, the substantive national dialogue on race and racism that Holder was pressing for never came to fruition due in no small part to President Obama's calculated decision to distance himself from Holder's comments. We say it was a "calculated" decision because Obama waited nearly a month after the controversy erupted—while conservative hounds were pressing full-throttle for Holder to apologize or resign and the media outlets, sensing a juicy scoop, were increasing their coverage of the story—before agreeing to discuss the matter publicly. Quieting the growing controversy and discrediting Holder's claims in the process, Obama declared in an interview with *New York Times* journalist Helene Cooper that the attorney general had spoken out of turn, that seeking common ground on social issues that cut across racial lines in the present rather than revisiting racial wounds of the past was a far more effective strategy for improving race relations. "I'm not somebody who believes that constantly talking about race somehow solves racial tensions," Obama asserted. "What solves racial tensions is fixing the economy, putting people to work, making sure that people have health care, [and] ensuring that every kid is learning out there" (p. A 26). Obama's message was clear. Race consciousness of the sort that Holder was advocating had no place on his post-racial political agenda—at least not a place that he was willing, at the risk of stirring up white anger, to acknowledge in the public domain. No doubt having received the response that they had pressed for—short of ousting Holder, that is—the conservative political hounds dropped the matter and the controversy-hunting media followed suit. Holder certainly didn't complicate matters. After the initial fall-out from the speech, he clammed up and offered no retort to his boss's public rebuke. Since making the comments and being reproached by the president, Holder has steered clear of such racial controversies, falling in line with Obama's post-racial approach and agenda. Apparently, even Holder overestimated how far our nation has come on race relations. Or, perhaps more accurately, he underestimated the degree to which racial politics dictated his boss's actions and behaviors, for, surely, Obama—careful politician that he is—was aware of Holder's racial politics when he handpicked him for the attorney general post.

These matters aside, if Holder's claim that our nation's treatment of African Americans and the poor is a barometer of our social and economic health as a nation, then there is a major cause for concern. In their op-ed article, "The Destruction of the Black Middle Class," acclaimed writer-activist Barbara Ehrenreich and inequality researcher-activist Dedrick Muhammad sound the alarm about the downward socioeconomic spiral of the black middle class. Debunking the widely held notion that the socioeconomic circumstances for the black middle class are steadily improving over time, Ehrenreich and Muhammad point to a study by Demos and the Institute for Assets and Social Policy, which reveals that at the start of our current recession—that officially began in December 2007—"33 percent of the black middle class was already in danger of falling out the middle class" (sec 4). For the black middle class, they write, the recession actually began in 2000. Between 2000 and 2007, "black employment decreased by 2.4 percent and incomes declined by 2.9 percent." During this stretch, "one third of black children lived in poverty and black employment—even among college graduates—consistently ran at about twice the level of white unemployment" (sec 5). When the current national recession took hold, it dramatically exacerbated an already dismal socioeconomic climate for blacks, igniting what the authors rightfully call a full-blown depression. The statistics certainly bear this out. According to the Bureau of Labor Statistics report, as of November 2009 the black unemployment rate was 15.7 percent and the Latino unemployment rate was 13.1 percent compared with 9.5 percent for whites.[2] In terms of lost wealth in the subprime loan debacle since the national recession began, blacks and Latinos have also been disproportionately disadvantaged: "According to the Center for Responsible Lending, Latinos will end up losing between $75 billion and $95 billion in home-value wealth from subprime loans, while blacks will lose between $71 billion and $92 billion" (sec 4). Even more alarming than these statistics is the staggering racial wealth gap between poor blacks and whites, which renders blacks more vulnerable during sharp economic downturns. Ehrenreich and Muhammad explain:

> In 1998, the net worth of white households on average was $100,700 higher than that of African Americans. By 2007, this gap had increased to $142,600. The Survey of Consumer Finances, which is supported by the Federal Reserve Board, collects this data every three years—and every time it has been collected, the racial wealth gap has widened. To put it another way: in 2004, for every dollar of wealth held by the typical white family, the African American family had only 12 cents. In 2007, it had exactly a dime. So when an African American breadwinner loses a job, there are usually no savings to fall back on, no well-heeled parents to hit up, no retirement accounts to raid. (sec 4)

Heading off claims that these alarming racial disparities are ultimately the fault of "cultural deficiencies" like black children born to single mothers, the authors note that the white two-parent family has declined more rapidly over the past four and a half decades than the black two-parent family. From 1960 to 2006, "black children living in a single parent home increased by 155 percent." Comparably, "white children living in single parent homes increased by a staggering 229 percent" (sec 3).

In his Oscar-winning global warming documentary *An Inconvenient Truth* former vice-president Al Gore used the analogy of a frog's reaction to dangerously hot water to stress the troubling tendency by those in power to wait until a problem has escalated to a cataclysmic point before acting to correct it. Put a frog directly in a pot of hot water, Gore explains, and it will register the danger immediately and jump out. However, if you put a frog in lukewarm water and slowly increase the temperature until boiling, the frog will not register the danger until it is too late to escape and save itself. This analogy works well to explain the race-informed social and economic crisis that is simmering to a boil now in the United States. Even though a population of black folks are doing well socially and economically in this country, they are unfortunately the exceptions not the rule. To view their success as evidence that "race" is no longer a major obstacle to socioeconomic upward mobility for blacks is to render invisible the reality that those who have "made it" have done so *despite* racial obstacles not because racial obstacles no longer exist. This is not to say that the racial climate for African Americans has not improved significantly in some ways over the past half century. Gone are Jim Crow segregation, laws barring blacks from voting, and state-sanctioned violence against blacks. Moreover, it is politically unfashionable now to openly support blatantly racist viewpoints and organizations like the Ku Klux Klan or Aryan Nations. In other words, the most overt signs of racial discrimination have all but disappeared from the public discourse. Remaining in its place, however, are institutionalized modes of racial discrimination or structural inequalities that continue to stymie most blacks' ability to move socially and economically beyond the imposed social and economic handicaps of the past. As the staggering statistics on black poverty and upper mobility reveal above, the grandchildren of Civil Rights–era blacks have not fared much better economically than previous generations and far worse—because of the prison industrial complex—in terms of criminality and incarceration rates. Indeed, one of the untold stories in the latter part of the twentieth century is how the emergence of the prison industrial complex coincided with the large-scale outsourcing of jobs and manufacturing bases by American companies. For this new generation of blacks, racism is experienced more abstractly—like having a "kick me" sign taped to one's back and being the butt of a mean joke that no one is willing to acknowledge. In a paradoxical and perhaps ironic way, the absence of visible and blatant markers of oppression becomes itself a menacing obstacle—the debilitating emotional and psychological consequences of which many African Americans of the Civil Rights generation have themselves yet to fully comprehend or appreciate.

Even though our title *Nation of Cowards: Black Activism in Barack Obama's Post-Racial America* riffs on Holder's controversial race speech —which we clearly find illuminating and timely—the chief aims of our study are not to validate Holder's claims. While we strongly agree with Holder's assertions that our nation reacts "cowardly" on issues of racial inequality/injustice and that it is a mistake to view Barack Obama's election as a sign that we are becoming a post-racial society, we are highly skeptical that Holder's proposed race talks will materialize without intense and organized activism from the African American community. What the Civil Rights Movement demonstrated on this score was that making overt racist practices uncomfortable and, to some degree, unprofitable (consider the Montgomery Bus Boycotts) was the key to forcing the dominant culture to change its behavior and repeal racially self-interested laws and policies. Martin Luther King Jr. underscores this sentiment in his famous "Letter From a Birmingham Jail," writing that "it is a historical fact that privileged groups seldom give up their privileges voluntarily." While it is not uncommon for privileged individuals to "see the moral light and voluntary give up their unjust [racial] posture," the privileged group as a whole tends to hold fast to power irrespective of the moral imperative. King concludes, "We know through painful experience that freedom is never voluntarily given by the oppressor; it must be demanded by the oppressed" ("Letter from a Birmingham Jail," 1896). In other words, to foster the kinds of substantive engagements with racial reality and black poverty specifically for which Holder calls, African Americans will have to shoulder the lion's share of the burden for initiating them. For reasons that we will explore in greater depth, black folks cannot rely on Barack Obama—or any leader for that matter—to do the heavy lifting of addressing racial inequality and injustice. Lamentable though it may be, if blacks do not take charge of their social and economic destiny—recalibrate their mindsets and demand through organized agitation that the dominant culture follow in tow—their circumstances on the ground will not improve and could, in all likelihood, become substantially worse.

We propose that to foster the kind of grassroots social movement necessary to press our nation and post-racial-minded president into action about these crucial race issues, African American communities must first get their house in order by having what we call "uncomfortable conversations" about longstanding, taboo cultural issues that inform and, at times, distort African Americans' thinking about political agency and self-determination. For these uncomfortable conversations to be useful and transformative, they must expose, challenge and, in some cases, explode the social terms on which black communities cope with extant white oppression and related acts of self-imposed victimization. Suffice it to say that a distinct, and perhaps inevitable, possibility exists that such conversations will be (mis)appropriated in the mainstream by political conservatives and/or many post-racial thinkers—including some blacks—to abdicate white culpability in African American suffering now and throughout history. The anxiety and frustration that this phenomenon of misappropriation engenders in African American communities cannot be overstated. In the final analysis, however, blacks cannot afford to let anxiety and frustration dictate the terms upon which they engage their social and economic circumstances. White denial of black suffering is not a new phenomenon. For instance, the dominant white mindset during the antebellum era—which is still widely held by many today—was that slavery was a benign and civilizing apparatus for enslaved Africans. Slavery is framed as the regrettable, but necessary, "cost" that blacks paid for Eurocentric modernization, for being "rescued" from a life of savagery and anarchy in Africa. This pattern of white denial will most likely persist whether or not African Americans are open about their problems or a black man resides in the White House. Given this reality, *Nation of Cowards* focuses more squarely on black agency and self-determination in the face of white denial. That is, we concentrate on what blacks can change about their behavior and thinking that will press whites into action on racial inequality and injustice. More specifically, we identify and seek to correct patterns of self-defeating behaviors that many blacks misconstrue as subversive or progressive. We call this pattern of behavior "self-imposed victimization." Examples of this behavior include elevating and defending as role models black athletes, entertainers, business moguls, and preachers whose self-interested, reckless, and irresponsible behaviors obstruct black empowerment and community building; embracing the black church's shift in the last forty years from the civil rights and human rights struggle to pro-capitalistic agendas; defending ineffective or corrupt black leadership in the name of political solidarity; and settling for white symbolic and empty gestures of racial progress rather than continuing to press for legislation that will empower us in quantifiable and meaningful ways.

Even as *Nation of Cowards* will engage African Americans as a group, we are acutely aware that there is not, nor has there ever been, a singular black experience or black perspective. In a word, African Americans are a very diverse group. Their experiences and perspectives are informed by a series of complex and intersecting variables, including class, social status, education, gender, sexuality, age, and religion. The key issue for us is that—despite this diversity of experience and perspective—race continues to be the *most* dominant and defining social variable for the overwhelming majority of Black America. As *Nation of Cowards* will demonstrate, even the most accomplished and successful among us are not completely insulated from the deleterious effects of racism. Indeed, one would be hard-pressed to find any black people, including the Obama family, whose lives have not been adversely affected by racial injustice; whose nuclear or extended family is not struggling with either poverty, incarceration, unemployment, poor mental or physical health, drug addiction, violence of one kind or another, or, in some cases, all of the above. This inescapable racial reality is precisely why so many black folks that have "made it," including the authors of this book, continue to press the issue of racial equality and justice.

We, the authors of this text, speak as one voice even as we have a unique set of academic specialties and personal experiences that we bring to bear on this important race debate. Though we both have strong scholastic backgrounds in African American studies, Ikard's field of expertise is African American literature with a focus on gender politics and popular culture studies, whereas Martell Teasley's field of expertise is social work with a focus on African American adolescent development, multicultural studies, Africana studies, and social policy. Ikard belongs to what cultural scholar Mark Anthony Neal refers to as the post-soul generation, and Teasley belongs to the baby boomer generation. We are fathers, sons, brothers, son-in-laws, community leaders, and scholar-activists. We are also first-generation college students, humanitarians, products of working-class communities, victims of racial profiling, and dedicated mentors. Ours is not simply an intellectual enterprise. The issues that we engage in this text have a direct impact on our lives and livelihoods and those of our children and loved ones. Though we offer potential remedies to the race-informed problems that we identify, we do not presume that ours are the only paths to accomplishing racial equality and justice. The problems we engage herein have long and complicated histories and are ever-shifting. Resolving them—or, at least, moving them toward resolution—will require long-term forward thinking. In other words, we view resolving these issues as a marathon campaign. No easy, quick fix solutions here.

To some, our focus on the adjustments that African Americans—the chief victims of white oppression—need to make regarding their racial mindsets and behavior may seem unfair, if not counterproductive. By taking ownership and responsibility for our victimization under white oppression, aren't we fundamentally letting white folks off the hook? Don't whites wield the bulk of social and economic power in the United States, and don't they continue to benefit, consciously and unconsciously, from institutionalized racial inequality? It goes almost without saying that whites should shoulder the bulk of the responsibility for righting the wrongs of their historical social, economic, and political injustices against blacks and oppressed groups. And, indeed, our history is littered with small, but significant, pockets of white leaders that have done just that, even to the point of social ostracism, beatings, imprisonment, and death. These white exceptions aside, it is certainly difficult—even with such a beautiful and accomplished black family now residing in the White House—to remain optimistic that racial inequality and injustice will be dismantled when the post-racial media blitz and President Obama's decidedly post-racial mindset and rhetoric are drowning out the true racial reality of America. But here's the rub—and this recalls a key point in Holder's speech—whites are not insulated from the deleterious effects of institutionalized racism. To invoke King again, "Injustice anywhere is a threat to justice everywhere. We [Americans] are caught in an inescapable network of mutuality, tied in a single garment of destiny. Whatever affects one directly, affects all indirectly" (1854). White studies provocateur Tim Wise speaks directly to this "inescapable network of mutuality" in *Between Barack and a Hard Place: Racism and White Denial in the Age of Obama* (2009), noting that whites across and within class lines pay a hefty price for institutionalized white privilege and blindness to African American suffering. He writes, "The racist bubble of white denial [of black suffering] and [white] privilege, which allows those of us called white to avoid dealing with the perceptions and realties of others, can leave us woefully ill-prepared when danger calls" (143). Invoking the tragic 9/11 attacks as a case in point, Wise asserts:

> It was virtually only whites who responded to the national trauma of the day by wondering aloud, in sight of television cameras and the world, *Why do they hate us?* That most whites have no clue as to the answer speaks volumes, for there

are few people of color who have the luxury of knowing it. Indeed, for blacks, and people of color more generally, survival has often depended upon having a keen sense of what others are thinking about them, and adjusting their lives accordingly. That whites have rarely if ever had to do this—to either think about how others might view them, or worry so much about how they were viewed as to actually change their behavior—may have served the privileged well up to this point, but in moments such as 9/11, that kind of ignorance can prove quite dysfunctional. (143)

Regarding socioeconomic issues, Wise argues that working-class whites who adhere to self-interested race thinking are ultimately operating against their best interests. Such thinking obscures both the commonality of class struggles that whites share with blacks and other oppressed groups and the egregiously lopsided class and power disparities that exist between whites. As such, working-class whites who "act on the basis of racial bonding and exclusion" become active, if not fully conscious, agents in fortifying "a politics of elite [class] domination" (415). They not only obliterate their chances of upward mobility now but for generations to come. Wise surmises that breaking this racialized pattern of white working-class self-sabotage will require "redefining white conceptions of self-interest from racial terms to economic ones" (145). More specifically, it will require whites to have substantive conversations about "how racial-interest thinking often stands in the way of true progress for all, regardless of color: how it has kept working people at each other's throats, fighting over the pieces of a [economic] pie that none of them, ultimately own; [and] how it has pitted white working class folks against immigrants of color and African Americans seeking greater opportunity for themselves and their families" (145).

Wise's argument recalls a personal anecdote famed novelist Ralph Ellison uses in his iconic essay "The World and the Jug" to take white critic Irvin Howe to task for insinuating in a scathing review of Ellison's *Invisible Man* that he knows better than Ellison and blacks what constitutes the real "black experience" of suffering and oppression in America. Whereas Ellison uses the anecdote more specifically to attack Howe's twisted racial claim that Richard Wright's protest novel *Native Son* (1940) is more "authentically" black than *Invisible Man*, we use it here to illustrate how blindness to white privilege and racial realities can potentially lead to dire outcomes for us all. The anecdote goes as follows: On a quail-hunting outing with his friend one snowy wintery day in Ohio, Ellison encounters a white man running toward them wielding a shotgun and shouting incoherently. Ellison's response to this racially charged incident—which we will quote at length here because of its political relevance—encapsulates the kind of racial illogic that continues to inform and complicate race relations today:

> He [the gun-toting white man] appeared as suddenly as the quail, and although the rifle was not yet to his shoulder, I was transfixed, watching him zooming up to become the largest, loudest, most aggressive-sounding white man I'd seen in my life, and I was, quite frankly, afraid. Then I was measuring his approach to the crunching tempo of his running and praying silently that he'd come within range of my shotgun before he fired; that I would be able to do what seemed necessary for me to do; that, shooting from the hip with an old twelve-gauge shotgun, I could stop him before he could shoot either me or my companion; and that, though stopped effectively, he would be neither killed, nor blinded, nor maimed.
>
> It was a mixed-up prayer in an icy interval which ended in a smoking fury of cursing, when, at a warning from my companion, the farmer suddenly halted. Then we learned that the reckless man had meant only to warn us off of land which was not even his but that of a neighbor—my companion's foster father. He stood there between two shotguns pointing short-ranged at his middle, his face quite drained of color now by the realization of how close to death he'd come, sputtering indignantly that we'd interpreted his rifle, which wasn't loaded, in a manner other than he'd intended. He truly did not realize that situations can be more loaded than guns and gestures more eloquent than words. (128–129)

Here, Ellison shows that the farmer's motives, however well intentioned, do not excuse him from blame. Ellison and his friend's initial interpretation of the white farmer's motives was filtered through a history of white male domination and violence against blacks generally and black men in particular; a history that the white farmer was most certainly aware even if he did not consider it relevant. Because of this racial history, it mattered little at the outset that the farmer's shotgun was not loaded or that his motive was to be helpful. Historical precedence dictated that Ellison and his friend could not risk miscalculating the farmer's motives. That the farmer is "indignant" at being "misinterpreted" by Ellison and his companion bespeaks the depths and dangers of his white privilege. As a white man the farmer is not obliged—socially or economically—to think critically about black realities or to take seriously how blacks might perceive him and whites. Despite not having to care about black realities and perceptions of whiteness, the farmer—as evidenced by his response of indignation—clearly *expects* Ellison and blacks to see his humanity beyond racial limits. This double-standard racial thinking puts the onus on Ellison and blacks to compensate and take responsibility for willful white blindness to oppressing blacks and exploiting white privilege. Ellison's "mixed-up prayer" reveals the extent to which racial inequality and disparities in power breeds fear and frustrates productive communication across racial lines. The sociopolitical stakes of this racial miscommunication are clearly higher for blacks and non-white ethnic minorities than they are for whites. If Ellison or his friend had acted on their initial fears and shot and killed the farmer, their fates would have been sealed. The best that they could have expected from such an outcome, especially during the 1950s when this incident occurred, was a long jail term. The more probable outcome would have been the death penalty for both, meted out vigilante style or through the justice system.

The huge chasms that still exist between black and white perceptions of the police and judicial system demonstrate that Ellison's racial calculus continues to play out, albeit in different ways, in U.S. society. The botched handling by the Bush administration of the mostly black and poor Katrina victims in New Orleans is a dramatic case in point. Subjected over an extended period of time to deplorable living conditions—including contending with uncared for and decaying bodies in living quarters, hostile police enforcement, excruciating heat, disease-infested waters, and water and food shortages—several individuals and groups began to act out in accordance with their inhumane treatment. Though the overwhelming majority of those stranded courageously endured the harrowing events without resorting to violence, the media began referring to them in thinly veiled racial terms as "refugees" and stories began to emerge from the ground that recalled age-old portraits of black immortality and primitivism. In a rather glaring example of this dynamic, two photos were released via Yahoo! News of stranded evacuees salvaging food from an abandoned grocery store. In one, a black man in waist-high water is shown carrying individual grocery items in one hand and a black plastic bag, presumably filled with groceries, in the other. In the next photo, a white couple is carrying groceries and wading through the same waters. Under the photograph of the black evacuee, the caption reads, "A young man walks through chest-deep flood water after *looting* a grocery store . . ." (Kinney). Under the other photograph with the white couple, however, the caption reads, "Two residents wade through chest-deep water after *finding* bread and soda from a local grocery store" (Kinney). According to an op-ed article "'Looting' or 'finding'?" on Salon.com, the company AFP/Getty Images that hired the white photographer, Chris Graythen, who took the infamous "finding" photo characterized the controversial backlash as regrettable, but explained away the caption as the result of strict professional protocol. Spokeswoman Bridget Russel told Salon.com reporter Aaron Kinney that, as a general rule, photographers only report what they can legitimately confirm. In this instance, she said Graythen didn't actually witness the whites looting and thus relayed as such in the photo. Kinney retorted, "But if he didn't witness an act of looting, how did Graythen determine where the items came from, or if they were "found"? Clearly at a lost to explain the discrepancy, Russel responded, "I wish I could tell you. . . . I haven't been able to talk to Chris" (Kinney). Was the white photographer Chris Graythen trying consciously to denigrate blacks and perpetuate white supremacy?[3] The answer is probably not. In fact, it is highly conceivable that race as such did not enter his consciousness when writing the caption for the photo. He and his employer's spokesperson Russel were innocent here in the same way as the farmer in Ellison's anecdote. Even though the collective intent of Graythen and AFP/Getty Images was presumably to offer an unbiased portrait of what was happening on the ground in New Orleans during the flooding, what materialized was a familiar racial narrative with real and dangerous consequences. Consider what happened several days into the recovery effort when the U.S. Army troops requested by Governor Kathleen Blanco from President George Bush arrived to restore order to the streets of New Orleans. Rather than serve as a comforting force for the harrowed, traumatized, and overwhelmingly black and poor citizens left behind in the city, the army swooped in primed for a violent altercation, their guns mounted high and aimed toward the American citizens and victims of state, local, and federal neglect in a clear display of military might and intimidation. A high-ranking black officer—Lt. Gen. Russel L. Honore[4]—captured headlines during this period when he was caught on camera chastising the troops—literally pushing their drawn weapons downward—for reacting to American citizens in this way.

A brief chapter summary of *Nation of Cowards* reveals how we plan to approach these and other pressing issues that have become decidedly more difficult for African Americans to identify and negotiate in Barack Obama's post-racial America. Chapter 1, "The Teaching Moment That Never Was: Henry Louis Gates, Barack Obama, and the Post-Racial Dilemma," engages the highly publicized arrest of prominent Harvard professor Henry Louis "Skip" Gates by a white officer, James Crowley, that erupted into a national controversy after President Obama intervened to support Gates and condemn longstanding patterns of racial profiling by the police and criminal justice system. We concentrate on the various ways that race defined and dictated the political and social terms on which Gates's arrest and, more generally, police brutality and racial profiling against blacks can be legitimately engaged in the public sphere. The pressing question for us is not *if* Crowley's actions against Gates or the white media backlash against Gates and Obama were racially informed and motivated, but how could we, as a race-obsessed nation, imagine that they could be otherwise. More broadly speaking, we examine the ways that accommodating (skewed) white expectations of black neutrality on race matters—meaning in this instance that blacks embrace responsibility for institutionalized racial inequality via post-racial/color-blind postures—reinforce the status quo, even in instances where the ultimate goal is to disrupt inequality. On this score, we argue that the reason that Obama, a former community organizer and social advocate for the black poor, so grossly underestimated white backlash is due largely to his romanticized post-racialist mindsets. Highlighting the ways that his mindset inadvertently reinforces normative whiteness and what historian David Roediger calls "colorblind *in*equalities" in the United States, we conclude that the political lessons that blacks should glean from this public controversy are that white post-racialist thinking is a new iteration of white supremacy. For this reason, blacks can ill-afford to use Obama as a model of black empowerment.

In chapter 2, "'I Know What's in His Heart': Enlightened Exceptionalism and the Problem with Using Barack Obama as the Racial Litmus

Test for Black Progress and Achievement," we engage how the phenomenon of what Wise calls "enlightened exceptionalism" allowed whites that still harbor racial stigmas about blacks to vote for Barack Obama for president. We contend that enlightened exceptionalism represents the new face of racism in the twenty-first century, affording many whites the opportunity to hold fast to their stereotypes about African Americans at large, while granting honorary whiteness to certain African Americans like Bill Cosby, Oprah Winfrey, and Barack Obama. Focusing on Obama's interventions in highly contentious race matters (particularly those involving white Democrats who have made racially insensitive comments in the public domain like Harry Reid and Joe Biden), we highlight how the president has manipulated the enlightened exceptionalism discourse in ways that, while advantageous to his political career, have hindered more than helped to explode stereotypes about the black poor.

Chapter 3, "The Audacity of Reverend Wright: Speaking Truth to Power in the Twenty-First Century," reconsiders the dominant view within and beyond black spaces that treats Reverend Wright as a hatemonger and lunatic black radical. We argue that Wright is neither crazy nor full of hate; rather, these imposed stigmas highlight the national cowardice that persists in addressing racial matters—past and present—openly and truthfully. Thus, we argue that Wright's true "transgression" for his white detractors was not—as was widely publicized—his supposedly anti-American views, but his direct confrontation of white racism and open condemnation of America's hypocritical promotion of democracy worldwide. Likewise, his true transgression for blacks was not his racial critique of American hypocrisy (for in this regard he had many supporters), but his refusal to pipe down and take the heat off of Obama at a crucial juncture during his Democratic presidential campaign against Hillary Clinton. Concomitantly, this chapter argues that Wright's propensity to "act up" in the pulpit and speak truth to power as it concerns struggling black communities (even if, at times, his claims are more conjectural than factual) is an asset rather than an obstacle to African American activism and empowerment in the twenty-first century. Even though Black America cheered Obama's successful navigation of the Wright controversy via his famous race speech, we contend that key political and ideological opportunities were lost. Namely, by accommodating the grand narrative of American (post-racial) exceptionalism and dismissing Wright (albeit without malice) as a relic of the past, Obama trivialized the persistence of racial inequities and, in so doing, cleared the way for the mainstream media to misrepresent the liberating and humanitarian legacy of activist black churches.

In chapter 4, "Setting the Record Straight: Why Barack Obama and America Cannot Afford to Ignore a Black Agenda," we examine the problems of Obama's conscious and politically expedient decision to forgo a black agenda. Using the contentious public spat over this issue between political commentator and television personality Tavis Smiley and political activist Al Sharpton as a touchstone, we argue that Americans in general and Black America in particular can ill afford to give Obama a free (racial) pass on this crucial national issue. In many ways, the Smiley/Sharpton debate symbolizes the unique challenge that Black America faces when holding the first black president accountable for a black agenda. While it is undeniable that Obama identifies with Black America and its plight for equality, he is, at bottom, wedded to a post-racial discourse that forecloses the possibility of openly endorsing policies that attack structural inequalities and illuminate the unique socioeconomic obstacles that plague Black American progress across class lines. Forwarding the argument that a black agenda is fundamentally an America agenda, we demonstrate that supporting a black president is not commensurate with cosigning all of his political objectives; that indeed it is our civic duty as Americans to hold him accountable, not just for the plight of Black America (his most loyal constituency), but for all disempowered citizens.

In chapter 5, "Pull Yourself Up By Your Bootstraps: Barack Obama, the Black Poor, and the Problems of Racial Common Sense Thinking," we discuss ways in which racialized thinking informs the maintenance of structural inequalities at the dawn of the twenty-first century, particularly during the Obama presidency. We are especially interested in addressing extant educational disparities for Black America, including their causality and tenacity. We engage a longstanding, if updated, version, of "racial common sense" thinking that informs Obama's mindset and rhetoric on such matters and that frustrates challenges to abate structural inequalities. "Racial common sense" in this context means compromising racial inequality for less than optimal outcomes. The thinking here is that accommodating elements of white power is the path of least resistance in acquiring social and economic gains. What we reveal is that such gains are already limiting, as they maintain rather than challenge the status quo. We end this chapter with a discussion of Harry Belafonte's insights on Black America's uncritical love affair with Obama and consider more broadly the political costs to Black America if we continue down this road with Obama and post-racial thinking.

What follows in *Nation of Cowards* is our attempt as humanitarians and proud citizens of the country to demand—as have many countless others across racial spectrums in the past—that our nation live up to its cherished democratic ideals. While it is important to acknowledge the strides that we have made in the past, it is equally, if not more important, to keep at the forefront how far we have yet to go. Acclaimed southern writer William Faulkner once wrote in *Requiem for a Nun*, "The past is never dead. It's not even past" (535). The reality is that a healthy society is always striving to come to terms with and to reconcile its past, however ugly or painful that past might be. As philosopher and essayist George Santayana reminds us in *Reason in Common Sense*, "Those who cannot remember the past are condemned to repeat it" (122). Historically speaking, Black America's relationship with White America reads like an abusive, codependent relationship. Repeatedly beaten and battered, made lofty promises of reform that rarely pan out to their advantage, asked not only to forgive such recurring trespasses but to forget they ever happened, Black America continues to return—arms wide open— to their abusive white partner; continues steadfastly to believe in an America Dream that has alluded all but an elite group of them for more than 230 years of our country's existence. As James Baldwin plainly puts it in his 1961 classic *Nobody Knows My Name*, "No one in the world . . . knows [white] Americans better or, odd as this may sound, loves them more than the American Negro. This is because he has had to watch you, outwit you, deal with you, even bear you, and sometimes even bleed and die with you, ever since we got here, that is, since both of us, black and white, got here—and this is a wedding" (220–221).

For many, Barack Obama's emergence and historic journey to become the first African American president seemed to signal that America had finally turned the corner on race relations, finally been vindicated for staying the course in a lopsided relationship that seemed always destined to end in heartbreak. When during the general election Michelle Obama opined candidly that "for the first time in my adult life I am proud of my country" (sec 3), the mainstream media and the McCain campaign pounced on the comment, insinuating that she and Obama, if not Black America at large, held questionable allegiances to this nation. The absurdity of the accusation was not lost on most African Americans. The white elite and chief historical benefactors of anti-democratic principles were casting aspersions at the beleaguered, true believers in the American Dream.

Fast forwarding to the end of President Obama's four years in office, we are beginning to see that the seemingly post-racial movement that catapulted him to the presidency was, if anything, a fleeting, post-racial moment. As the intense racial flare-ups in his young tenure as president have already demonstrated, Barack Obama cannot talk candidly about race and racism without taking heat from virtually all angles. Savvy politician that he is, Obama has adjusted his rhetoric and agenda accordingly, abandoning in totality what was already an admittedly soft political stance on racism. As far as race relations are concerned, then, Black America finds itself in an eerily, familiar position. The post-racial dream that many latched on to during Obama's improbable run to the White House—that indeed many still cling to now—is turning out be another dream deferred. But, alas, African Americans have plenty of experience as an oppressed people with broken promises, unmet expectations, and anointed leaders that ultimately disappoint. And, perhaps, that's the problem. African Americans have become too desensitized to their subordinate social status, ballooning incarceration rates, substandard educational opportunities, and extant token representations in the halls of power. To this point, ethnographer Jon Jackson relays in his book *Racial Paranoia* (2008) that "contrary to some common reactionary assumptions about a supposedly self-pitying embrace of victimhood within the black community, the ultimate trump card for such a position, chattel slavery, is hardly something . . . that black Americans dwell on—or even bring up. Far from using it as a crutch, they barely discuss it most of the time." Jackson opines that this silence is perhaps

a coping mechanism "to fend off any twinges of humiliation or emas-
culation" (47).

Whether blacks are avoiding the subject of slavery because of pain,
fear, apathy, or a combination of all three, the twisted irony is that they—
like their white counterparts—want to move beyond a historical past
that they have, at best, a cursory knowledge and, at worse, no substantive
knowledge at all. Truth is, until we as a nation are willing to confront our
cowardice and grapple collectively with this painful history, we cannot
realistically expect to achieve a post-*racist* society or reconcile the lingering racial tensions that explode violently to the surface of our national
consciousness during catastrophes like the Los Angeles riots, the Hur-
ricane Katrina fallout in New Orleans, and the Trayvon Martin controversy. Perhaps the biggest travesty of this racial calculus is that the onus
for fostering this uncomfortable interracial conversation is displaced
onto the shoulders of African Americans. What the dominant culture
has yet to fully grasp—especially the working-class masses—is that they
have as much to lose in resisting this uncomfortable conversation as
African Americans. And, here again, Baldwin puts our interracial American predicament into perspective: "Whether I like it or not, or whether
you like it or not, we [blacks and whites in the U.S.] are bound together
forever. We are part of each other. What is happening to every Negro in
the country at any time is also happening to you. There is no way around
this" (221). As *Nation of Cowards* will demonstrate, Black America is the
proverbial canary in the coalmines of America's cultural consciousness
and socioeconomic prosperity. If the health of Black America falters,
the rest of America will soon follow. And none of us can afford for that
to happen.

# 1

## The Teaching Moment That Never Was

*Henry Louis Gates, Barack Obama,*
*and the Post-Racial Dilemma*

WHEN DISTINGUISHED black Harvard professor Henry Louis "Skip" Gates was arrested at his Cambridge, Massachusetts, residence for disorderly conduct on July 16, 2009, by James Crowley, a white police officer, the story seemed at once familiar and unique. Familiar in the sense that African Americans in general and African American men in particular have a long and ugly history with the police force and judicial system, dating back to slavery. Unique in the sense that the black man, Gates, in this familiar racial theater was wealthy and possessed "real" power and agency to fight back on an individual level.[1] (It also didn't hurt that Gates had friends in high places, including the first black president of the United States.) Indeed, it is highly likely that many, if not most, black men today older than twenty-five have at least one police brutality or mistreatment story to tell. What made this instance unique, then, was not the fact that it involved a rich and powerful black man who was up against a status quo police force, but that when push came to shove, as the black colloquium goes, Gates was able to wield his considerable influence to gain a public hearing on the matter and pressure the Cambridge judicial system to drop the charges without having to, say, organize a mass demonstration or go on a hunger strike.

Though in the national race narrative Gates has often been characterized as what John McWhorter calls "a professional racebaiter," those of us who are familiar with Gates's scholarship and political outlook recognize that nothing could be further from the truth. In "Skip Gates and the Post-Racial Project," Melissa Harris-Perry rightly notes that despite residing over the preeminent institution of African American studies Gates "is no race warrior seeking to right the racial injustices of the world." Rather his modus operandi[2] is to "be a collector of black talent, intellect, art, and achievement" (online). Noting Gates's tendency to compare himself to "race man" and intellectual giant W. E. B. Du Bois, Harris-Perry asserts as a matter of clarity that Gates resembles Du Bois only to the degree that he emphasizes the importance of studying black culture. Characterizing Gates favorably as the embodiment "of a kind of post-racialism," Harris-Perry contends that Gates is "enamored" with the "American [racial diversity] project," not disillusioned with it as some popular media outlets have claimed. Gates, in other words, is no race man or activist-scholar. He has been popping his "post-racial" collar for quite some time. Even the black neoconservative John McWhorter has come to Gates's defense. In his essay, "Gates Is Right—and We're Not Post-Racial Until He's Wrong," McWhorter writes that the "idea that [Gates] should have exhibited 'deference to the police' [even though he was rightfully justified in being upset by the interrogation] ignores the totemic status that black men's encounters with the police have in the [public consciousness]. . . . There's a reason Gates told the *Washington Post* . . . that what happened to him was part of a 'racial narrative,' and that awareness surely informed his angry conduct. The relationship between black men and police forces is, in fact, the main thing keeping America from becoming 'post-racial' in any sense" (online).

What appeared obvious to a good many African Americans who followed the public controversy, including President Obama, was that even if Gates was "unruly" and "hostile," as Crowley claims in his police report and which, for the record, Gates vehemently refutes, he had good cause to be. Gates, who essentially was minding his own business at his residence, became the focal point of police suspicion in large part because of his race. The exclusive, upper-class Cambridge neighborhood in which Gates resides is predominantly white. While it is not difficult to imagine why President Obama felt compelled to wade into this controversy, it almost goes without saying that he grossly underestimated the limitations of his ability—even as a self-branded post-racialist—to openly condemn institutional racism. Given that he had only recently been able to turn the racial controversy involving his relationship with his former pastor Rev. Jeremiah Wright, an unapologetic race man, and Trinity United, a progressive black nationalist–leaning church, into a bonanza for his campaign in his now famous "race speech," one can imagine that Obama felt confident in his race-mediator-in-chief status. This is not to say that Obama acted without weighing the political cost of intervening. Obama only entered the fray *after* the Cambridge police department dropped all charges against Gates. Moreover, the president was defending the "Barack Obama of black studies," if you will.[3] As previously noted, Gates was no lightning rod on race matters. If anything, Gates has taken heat within and beyond black intelligentsia for his post-racialist perspectives on a wide range of race matters.[4] It appears, then, that President Obama was banking that Gates's reputation as a post-racialist and race relations mediator and, no doubt, his own cultural clout on similar grounds, would neutralize any political blowback and perhaps even foster a productive dialogue on racial profiling and policing. He was clearly mistaken.

To borrow journalist Ellis Cose's terminology, we continue to live in a "race-obsessed" society; our very notions of reality and even who qualifies as human are refracted through a dominant prism of race. Thus, in this chapter we will concentrate on the various ways that race defined and dictated the political and social terms on which these issues could be legitimately engaged in the public sphere. The pressing question for us is not *if* race mattered in this national fiasco but rather how race mattered. Moving from the general to the specific in terms of how African Americans can productively navigate such complex and ever-changing race-obsessed thinking, we consider the ways that Obama's decidedly post-racial postures overdetermine black agency and box him in politically on matters of racial inequality. The fact that Obama, a former community organizer and social advocate for the black poor, so grossly underestimates the explosive (white) outcomes of his comments on Gates demonstrates in dramatic fashion the pitfalls of post-racial postures in a race-obsessed society.

TEACHABLE MOVEMENTS ON RACE
IN AMERICA: FOR BLACKS ONLY?

Fielding a question about the Gates/Crowley incident during a press
conference touting his new healthcare reform initiatives, Obama opined
with light humor, interspersed with his customary measured and con-
ciliatory tone, that the circumstances were regrettable and that, without
having all the facts at his disposal, he couldn't speak to "what role race
played in" Gates's arrest. He then added famously:

> But I think it's fair to say, number one, *any of us* would be pretty angry; number
> two, that the Cambridge police acted stupidly in arresting somebody when there
> was already proof that they were in their own home. And number three, what I
> think we know separate and apart from this incident is that there is a long history
> in this country of African-Americans and Latinos being stopped by law enforce-
> ment disproportionately. That's just a fact. (*Chicago Sun-Times*, my emphasis)

Reminiscent of the skewed fixation and parsing out of Eric Holder's
"nation of cowards" comment, the media locked in on Obama's characterization of the Cambridge police as having "acted stupidly" in arresting
Gates after determining that he was the rightful occupant of the home
and not a burglar. Virtually overnight, the national narrative shifted
from a focus on Gates, Crowley, and racial profiling to Obama's (mis)
handling of a sensitive national racial matter. Indeed, a Pew Survey taken
at the time revealed that 79 percent of the public was aware of Obama's
comments on the incident. The poll data also revealed that Obama's
"approval ratings fell among non-Hispanic whites over the course of the
interviewing period as the focus of the Gates story shifted from details
about the incident to Obama's remarks about the incident" (Pew). Before
the story shifted to Obama's remarks, his approval rating among non-
Hispanic whites was 53 percent. Afterwards, it fell to 46 percent. And,
even though the nation was largely split about who was at fault in the
Gates/Crowley incident as noted above, "more people disapprove (41%)
than approve (29%) of the president's handling of the situation. And by
a margin of about two-to-one, more whites disapprove (45%) than approve (22%)" (Pew).

While technically Obama never apologized outright for making
his remarks, he initiated a public relations campaign, booking inter-

views with all the major television networks, wherein he voiced regret over his choice of words in characterizing Crowley and the Cambridge Police Department as having "acted stupidly" in arresting Gates. He also dramatically shifted gears on assigning blame, noting that both men probably overreacted. Retreating back to his hallmark colorblind racial discourse, Obama—via a suggestion by Crowley—invited both men and their families to the White House to iron out their differences civilly over a beer. The media-branded "Beer Summit," which Obama represented (this time from the familiar position of race mediator rather than race instructor) as the teachable moment to the nation, amounted to little more than a public relations gesture to tamp down the media frenzy. Vice President Joe Biden even made a guest appearance, an appearance that was described without irony in the *New York Times* as "add[ing] balance to the photo op" ("Over Beers, No Apologies, but Plans to Have Lunch").

Let's begin our examination of the racial challenges of Obama's presidency and the problems of his post-racial thinking and politics by harkening back to the rousing speech on black self-determination that he delivered to the NAACP Centennial Convention in New York the very day that his friend Gates was arrested. Obama urges his mostly upscale and affluent black audience to abandon victim-centric narratives that tie our present socioeconomic crisis to historical patterns of white oppression. Of particular note is a segment of the speech in which Obama veers from his prepared text and launches into a black preacherly cadence, admonishing the NAACP and African Americans to revamp their mind-sets about combating structural inequality. Signifying culturally on the longstanding African American belief that the federal government is chiefly responsible for righting the historical wrongs of white oppression against blacks, Obama sermonizes:

> Government plans alone won't get our children to the Promised Land. We need a new mind set, a new set of attitudes—*because one of the most durable and destructive legacies of discrimination is the way we've internalized a sense of limitations;* how so many in our community have come to expect so little from the world and from themselves. We've got to say to our children, yes, if you're African American, the odds of growing up amid crime and gangs are higher. Yes, if you live in a poor neighborhood, you will face challenges that somebody in a wealthy suburb does not have to face. But that's not a reason to get bad grades . . .

that's not a reason to cut class . . . that's not a reason to give up on your education
and drop out of school . . . No one has written your destiny for you. *Your destiny
is in your hands—you cannot forget that.* That's what we have to teach all of our
children. No excuses . . . No excuses. You get that education, *all those hardships
will just make you stronger, better able to compete.* Yes we can.

　　To parents . . . we can't tell our kids to do well in school and then fail to support them when they get home. . . . You can't just contract out parenting. For our
kids to excel, we have to accept our responsibility to help them learn. That means
putting away the Xbox . . . [and] putting our kids to bed at a reasonable hour. . . .

　　*We need to go back to the time, back to the day when we parents saw . . . some kid
fooling around and it wasn't your child, but they'll whup you anyway. . . . Or at least
they'll tell your parents. . . . That's the meaning of community. That's how we can
reclaim the strength and the determination and the hopefulness that helped us come
so far; helped us make a way out of no way.* (online, my emphasis)

At first glance, Obama's tough-love, sermonic meditation on black
self-determination and empowerment seems productive, if not altogether self-evident. Given the crumbling state of the black nuclear family, the low academic achievement rates compared to whites, and the
high rates of black male incarceration, who can argue against the pressing need for black folks to identify and correct self-destructive behavior, especially in regards to parenting and education? The problem with
Obama's portrait of Black America and his rousing racial call-to-action
is, to borrow Lani Guinier's phrasing, "history does matter" when examining structural inequalities and developing strategies to combat them.
Though on its face, Obama's speech seems historically grounded (in the
early part of his speech he recalls the social obstacles of slavery and Jim
Crow segregation) his narrative pivots on a familiar suffering-makes-
you-stronger refrain that obscures the myriad obstacles to black self-
determination, on the one hand, and lets whites off the hook for past and
present black oppression, on the other. The notions of black self-determination that Obama advocates for in his speech, describing them as a
"new mindset" and "new set of attitudes," are, in fact, longstanding ideas
about racial uplift rendered through a conservative framework. It is not
inconsequential, then, that Obama's "new" mindset and attitudes beckon
that we return to a romanticized cultural moment "back in the day" when
we supposedly placed a higher premium on community and moral values
and helped raise and discipline each others' children. Crucially missing
from this romanticized portrait, of course, are the socioeconomic fac-

tors like the common experience of overt racism that pressed disparate classes of black folks together out of political and social necessity, culminating into the twentieth-century Civil Rights Movement. Obama's nostalgic rhetorical gesture here, which also subtly plays up the skewed notion that the current "hip hop generation" of African Americans are largely to blame for failing black communities, shifts the debate over black self-determination from the historical and social domain to that of the personal. Consider the ways that Obama describes the mindset of black self-defeatism. He writes, "the most durable and destructive legacies of discrimination is the way *we've* internalized a sense of limitations" (Sweet, my emphasis). Rather than acknowledge that whites have historically fortified this mindset via slavery, Jim Crow segregation, and other orchestrated forms of oppression, Obama shifts the blame rhetorically onto African Americans. In his formulation, only African Americans are raced and have the responsibility to alter the course of history. Whiteness and, indeed, the causality of white oppression are ultimately rendered invisible as if whites have no racial history or a direct stake in maintaining the structural inequalities linked to slavery, Jim Crow segregation, and the like.

What this rhetorical erasure of white culpability in oppressing blacks communicates to Americans in general and African Americans in particular is that Black America has somehow arrived at this point of socioeconomic crisis due, in large part, to *their* failure to see past systemic white oppression. To wit, Obama tells us "not to forget" that "Your destiny is in your hands." He then follows up with, "You get that education, all those hardships will just make you stronger, better able to compete" (Sweet). Not only does the issue of white culpability fall out of the racial equation for achieving black self-determination and empowerment but also the notion that blacks, and by extension our nation as a whole, should view oppression as ultimately a serious obstacle to black achievement and social equality. Flowing rhetorically like a cleverly updated version of Booker T. Washington's "Atlanta Exposition Address" in which he beckons blacks to view the hardships of slavery as an opportunity for social and moral growth, Obama reifies the *racist* post-racial argument that blacks who demand quantifiable white accountability for present-day structural inequalities (like those that call for reparations for slavery) are somehow backward thinking. Moreover, Obama steers the discourse of racial empowerment toward romanticized and symbolic domains and away from hardcore strategies to obliterate the structural barriers that continue to hamper black upward mobility and fortify poverty.

## THE "RACE SPEECH" AND PACIFYING WHITES

In terms of a political strategy to get elected to the presidency, the post-racialist rhetoric that Obama rehearses at the NAACP Centennial Convention has proven quite effective. Indeed, Obama's political calling card was his hyperconciliatory rhetoric on race; rhetoric that, at once, substantiated white notions that black self-determination was not hindered by white victimization (as mentioned above) and projected that a post-racial mindset in the United States was not only possible but ideologically inevitable. To be fair to Obama on this score, the radically raced climate in the country largely dictated that as an African American he had to tread lightly on the issue of racial inequality so as not to offend his white constituency; thus, in many ways, while teachable moments concerning issues of race may be *for* all Americans, they can only be *about* black Americans.

As we witnessed throughout his historic and trailblazing political campaign, Obama strategically skirted the issue of race and racism whenever possible. And usually when he did discuss race, it was either to admonish blacks generally and black men specifically to take stronger ownership of self-determination—especially in relation to childrearing, education, and criminality—or to highlight the socioeconomic strides we have made as a nation toward racial equality. Even when Obama was pressed into giving a speech on race during the heated Democratic primaries after explosive clips surfaced of his longtime church pastor and mentor Rev. Jeremiah Wright seeming to portray the United States as unforgivably racist, he avoided the racial trap of looking like an angry black man to whites and an impotent accommodationist to blacks by blaming Wall Street greed and Washington political corruption— not historical white oppression—for corrupting black/white relations. Though in his speech he broached the issue of slavery and its lasting socioeconomic on blacks, he strategically shifted the conversation from macro and longstanding patterns of racial oppression and toward micro issues and personal narratives. His overriding political message was that we should hate the sin of racism—practiced on both sides of the black/white color line—but not the sinner. He argued that keeping these variables separate allows us to see and appreciate each other's humanity beyond the flaws of our racial stereotypes and the lingering pain of our tumultuous racial history. In this narrative, Wright emerged as a good and patriotic man at heart who had regrettably allowed the sin of past racial wounds to fester into cynicism and cloud his judgment. Giving balance to his racial narrative, Obama invoked his white grandmother Madelyn Dunham as another case in point. He notes that she possessed an irrational fear of black men even as she openly embraced Obama and her black son-in-law. In Obama's formulation, to vilify Wright and Dunham as racist hatemongers on the sole basis of their regrettably racist attitudes was to vilify the country and ourselves. His chief point being that we are all complicit on some level in sustaining America's racial drama. While the speech proved wildly effective, virtually squashing the Wright controversy overnight (even though another flare-up by the indomitable Wright pressed Obama to break ties with his spiritual mentor altogether) and prompting comparisons in the media to the greatest political speeches in U.S. history, it also served to further box in Obama politically on the issue of race. It fostered the expectation, especially for his post-racially minded white voters, that a color-blind approach was the *only* legitimate and constructive way for Obama and Black America to engage racial matters.

That Obama was caught off guard by the controversy and media blitz sparked by his comments about Gates and the "stupid-acting" Cambridge police demonstrates, on one level, the irreconcilability between his self-branding as a post-racialist and his political agitation against overt racial inequality. The unspoken bargain Obama made with post-racialist thinking White America, including whites who did not vote for him, basically blew up in his face. A blog comment by a self-described staunch white Obama supporter using the online tag "KJ White" illustrates how this broken bargain played out for many of his core white constituency. KJ White chastises Obama for taking racial sides on this controversy by supporting Gates, explaining that this was a no-win so-lution for him because ultimately culpability is in the eyes of the be-holder. Offering her own version of a balanced racial critique, she argues that "different people will look at the Gates situation and SEE different things," depending on their racial vantage point. Extending validity to both extreme racial perspectives on the controversy, she concludes that Gates and Crowley were equally culpable. She then admonishes Obama, "The country WANTS more than anything to get beyond these kinds of incidents. The country is TRYING. That is why they voted for Obama! This kind of stuff is the LAST thing we need" (online). Though KJ White obviously lacks the rhetorical sophistication of Obama, her rationale—which is woefully ahistorical in scope—grows out of a similar racial calculus that Obama employed during his presidential campaign, in his handling of Eric Holder's race speech, at the NAACP Centennial conven-tion, and toward transparently xenophobic groups like the Birthers[5] and Tea Party Patriots.[6] The symbolic capital of Obama as the paragon of ra-cial transcendence is unmistakable. KJ White's thinking is that race as a significant factor of experience and treatment is no longer relevant; the election of a black man to the office of the presidency was fundamental proof of this new reality. Obama was ultimately at fault for KJ White because, rather than reject the idea that race was a significant factor in this circumstance, he "took sides" and thus inflamed more racial divisive-ness. In short, her message to Obama is that he let his white voters down by expressing his cultural blackness.

As his dramatic backpedaling on his characterization of Crowley and the Cambridge Police Department demonstrated, Obama clearly internalized the message from his white constituency. It is hardly a con-sequence, then, that when the next major "racial test" came along—South Carolina Republican congressman Joe Wilson shouting out "You lie!" during a presidential address before the U.S. Congress—Obama reverted conspicuously to his branded post-racial posture. When former president Jimmy Carter weighed in on the situation and tagged Wil-son's behavior racist—a conclusion that drew the support of staunch liberal post-racialists like *New York Times* journalist Maureen Dowd and even inspired a parody against Wilson on *Saturday Night Live*—Obama strongly rejected these conclusions and urged Congress and the public at large to drop the matter altogether.[7] In a related controversy, he also categorically rejected the idea that race was a factor in the unruliness of the town hall meetings on healthcare taking place across the nation where protestors often waved posters portraying Obama as Hitler and an African Witch Doctor.

Looking back at Obama's controversial comments about Gates and the Cambridge Police Department, we begin to see the true cost of post-racial thinking to black folks in particular. Because of whites' preoccupation with Obama's support of Gates and indictment of the Cambridge police, the most substantive aspects of Obama's comments regarding racial profiling and criminal justice system fell completely off the media radar. Following the infamous statement concerning the "stupid" behavior of the Cambridge police, Obama asserts,

> What I think we know separate and apart from this incident is that there is a long history in this country of African-Americans and Latinos being stopped by law enforcement disproportionately. That's just a fact.
>
> As you know, . . . when I was in the state legislature in Illinois, we worked on a racial profiling bill because there was indisputable evidence that blacks and Hispanics were being stopped disproportionately. And that is a sign, an example of how, you know, race remains a factor in the society.
>
> That doesn't lessen the incredible progress that has been made. I am standing here as testimony to the progress that's been made. And yet the fact of the matter is, is that, you know, this still haunts us.
>
> *And even when there are honest misunderstandings, the fact that blacks and Hispanics are picked up more frequently, and often time for no cause, casts suspicion even when there is good cause.* And that's why I think the more that we're working with local law enforcement to improve policing techniques so that we're eliminating potential bias, the safer everybody's going to be. (Sweet)

What most people don't know and what, indeed, the popular media was negligent in making known, was that in 2002, while a senator in Illinois, Obama had been a major player in passing an ostensible anti-racial profiling legislation that mandated the collection of data on the race and ethnicity of all motorists stopped by the police. According to Harvey Grossman, legal director of the ACLU of Illinois, the data collected from the study in 2008 revealed "that African American drivers in Illinois are 25 percent more likely to be stopped and Hispanic drivers are 10 percent more likely to be stopped than white drivers" (online). Additionally, the data showed that after black and Hispanic drivers were stopped for routine traffic violations, they were far more likely than whites to be asked for "consent" to search their vehicles. Grossman explains, "These searches are performed when there is no articulable suspicion of wrong-doing and are at the complete discretion of the police" (online). He notes that in 2006 the Illinois State Police "were twice as likely to ask an African American driver for permission to search his car and four times more likely to ask a Hispanic driver for permission to search when compared with white motorists" (online). When an independent consultant hired by the Illinois State Police reviewed the data, the finding was "that there was no innocent explanation for the disparate treatment of minorities once they are stopped for a routine traffic infraction" (online). The rub is that "the data collected actually show that police are more likely to find contraband in the smaller percentage of white motorists they search, compared with the higher percentage of minority motorists subjected to this humiliating treatment. Despite claims that consent searches are an important law enforcement 'tool,' the data reveal that for calendar year 2007, as an example, no significant amount of drugs were found in a consent search performed by the Illinois State Police" (online).

Contrary to the (white) public perception that Obama was "picking sides" and speaking out of turn on the issue, he was, in fact, *uniquely* qualified to speak to these issues of racial profiling in the criminal justice system. Not only had Obama witnessed racial profiling by the police with his own eyes—an issue he engages directly in his memoir *Dreams of My Father* (2004)—but he also had firsthand experience as a legislator crafting policies that helped identify and combat the longstanding practice. There is no doubt that Obama underestimated the politics of his cultural blackness in speaking out in favor of Gates and against the (mostly white) Cambridge Police Department. That Obama delivered his comments at the press conference on healthcare in a jocular and light-hearted way—a far cry from his no-holds barred, preacherly rhetoric in his NAACP speech—reveals he was aware, at least on some level, that he was treading on a potentially explosive subject even if he ultimately believed that white Americans would respond positively to his message. As it turned out, he wasn't nearly as aware as he should have been about the low level of racial tolerance in America, a situation made all the more combustible by the tenacity of his brand as a post-racialist president.

We should view the national racial controversy that blew up around Gates's arrest as, above all, a warning against constructing empowerment and resistant strategies squarely on racial idealism. This is not to say that discourses of inspiration and hope are inherently bankrupt. If properly wedded to substantive strategies of social reform—as we have witnessed throughout the history of black struggle in the United States—such discourses can prove quite effective. The problem emerges, however, when we confuse our idealism with the material reality of living in a raced-obsessed society. Renowned writer and essayist Ralph Ellison touches on this phenomenon in "Harlem Is Nowhere" when he expounds on why so many blacks who migrated from the South to Harlem during the post–World War I era experienced psychotic breaks. Believing falsely that Harlem offered a genuine opportunity for them to live out the mythical American Dream, many blacks abandoned what Ellison calls their "peasant cynicism" when they fled the Jim Crow South. Ellison describes "peasant cynicism" as a conscious "refusal to hope for the fulfillment of hopeless hopes," a state of mind that provides a sense of emotional security "gained from confronting and accepting . . . the obscene absurdity of [one's racial] predicament" in America (298). In letting their psychic racial guards down, black southerners opened the door to the emotional and psychological crisis that results from not having an adequate critical apparatus from which to negotiate the "obscene absurdity" of racial illogic in the United States.

Though the cultural landscape has shifted in substantial ways since Ellison wrote this essay in 1948, his analysis of the psychic predicament of Black America still holds true in many regards. Maintaining a high level of skepticism about racial progress is, in fact, a healthy critical posture given the extant realities of structural inequality in the country. In truth, electing a black president has in some ways made it more—not less—difficult to engage the racial components of structural inequality, a lesson that both Gates and Obama learned the hard way. In all likelihood, we probably won't see either of them venture down this bumpy racial road again, at least not any time soon. Regrettably, the rest of us, especially blacks at the bottom rungs of society, do not have the luxury of following their lead. The stakes for our socioeconomic health and well-being are simply too high to lay low. In their underground hit "Politrickkks" rap group Dead Prez riffs on the intraracial idea that voting for Barack Obama constitutes a major step toward black empowerment. They wax poetically, "I don't want to discourage my folk [from voting for Obama] / I believe in hope/ *I just want us to want more*" ("Politrickkks," my emphasis). And, therein lies the crux of the problem. If we truly want to alter our fortunes, we have to "want more" than the symbolic capital of having a black family in the White House, however hopeful that makes us feel, and do more than rant within our communities about racial profiling and structural inequality, however daunting it may seem to stand up against the police and social injustice.

In the final analysis, teachable moments about race in America will only have real utility when both whites and blacks (and for that matter all racial and ethnic groups) face up to the impact that race and racism continue to have on our society. As the Gates controversy demonstrated in rather dramatic fashion, the election of Barack Obama as the 44th president did not mark the end of racial oppression or structural inequalities in the United States. Certain issues of race are as explosive now as they have ever been. While political optimism has its place, it is hard to put too much stock in the reality that it is now possible for a black man to be elected to the presidency when a significant segment of the black community remains unemployed, undereducated, overrepresented in prison, and cemented in poverty. As a general rule of history, challenging status quo power hierarchies—which perpetuate blacks' subordinate socioeconomic status—has always proven to be a risky and dangerous enterprise, especially for those within black communities with the fewest resources and political clout. But, to riff on the words of an old Negro spiritual, nobody said that the road to equality would be easy. One thing is for sure; African Americans are not going to "hope" or "PBS-special" their way to solutions to the problems plaguing our communities. "When you Pray," goes the ancient African proverb, "move your feet."

# 2

## "I Know What's in His Heart"

*Enlightened Exceptionalism and the Problem with
Using Barack Obama as the Racial Litmus Test for
Black Progress and Achievement*

BARELY A YEAR into Barack Obama's presidency, Senate Majority Leader Harry Reid captured national headlines when his pre-election perspective on Obama's chances of becoming the nation's first black president came to light. Seeking to generate interest in their then up-coming book *Game Change* (which chronicles the behind-the-scene maneuvering during the 2008 campaign), journalists Mark Halperin and John Heilemann released a juicy excerpt in which Reid expresses his belief that America was ready for a black president and that Senator Barack Obama fit the bill perfectly. What landed Reid in hot water was his qualifying statement about the aspects of Obama's "blackness"—physically and culturally speaking—that would be especially appealing to white voters. These qualities included the fact that Obama was "light-skinned" and spoke "with no Negro dialect, unless he wanted to have one" (36). Predictably, the GOP establishment, including the newly elected and first black RNC chairman Michael Steele, went on the attack, accusing Reid of being racially insensitive and calling for him to resign. Moreover, they accused the Democratic Party—who rallied around Reid—as having a double standard on matters of race and racism. Had a Republican senator and majority leader used such language to characterize Barack Obama or blacks, they argued, Democrats would be calling for his or her head. Most of the air was taken out of the story quickly, of course, because Barack Obama accepted Reid's proffered public and private apology—issued almost immediately after the story first broke—without hesitation. More specifically, Obama announced in a White House press release, that he accepted Reid's "apology without question because I've known him for years, I've seen the passionate leadership he's shown on issues of social justice and I know *what's in his heart*. As far as I'm concerned, the book [on this controversy] is closed" (Holland, my emphasis). He reiterated his feelings more strongly in an interview with black CNN commentator Roland Martin, saying Reid "is a good man who's always been on the right side of history. For him to have used some inartful language in trying to praise me, and for people to try to make hay out of that makes absolutely no sense. He apologized, recognizing that he didn't use appropriate language, but there was nothing mean-spirited in what he had to say" (online).

Reid's controversial racial comments and, indeed, Obama's apologist response to them, recall the controversy during the kickoff of the Democratic presidential primaries when Senator Joe Biden described Obama as the first "mainstream African American [presidential candidate] who is articulate and bright and clean and a nice-looking guy" (Balz). When Obama was later asked if he took offense to Biden's comments, he opined, "I have absolutely no doubt about *what is in his heart* and the commitment he's made to racial equality in this country" (Sargent, my emphasis). Obama "closed the book" on Biden's suspect racial attitude in most dramatic fashion: he tapped Biden to be his running mate in the general election.

If, as the old political adage goes, a "gaffe" in Washington is when a politician slips up and tells the truth, then there is much more to Reid's and Biden's comments about Obama than meets the eye. Indeed, the racial thinking that undergirds both Reid's and Biden's praise of Barack Obama's talents is what white antiracist scholar-activist Tim Wise refers to as "enlightened exceptionalism." Essentially an updated version of white supremacy, enlightened exceptionalism allows whites

> to carve out acceptable space for individuals such as Obama who strike them
> as different, as exceptions who are not like the rest. That this "enlightened
> exceptionalism" manages to accommodate individual people of color, even as
> it continues to look down upon the larger mass of black and brown America
> with suspicion, fear, and contempt, suggests the fluid and shape-shifting nature

of racism. It indicates that far from vanishing, racism has become more so-
phisticated and that Obama's rise could, at least in part, stem from the triumph
of racism, albeit of a more seeming ecumenical type than that to which we have
grown accustomed. (23)

Whites who espouse this viewpoint feel "enlightened," then, because they experience this pattern of distinguishing exceptional blacks
from the "herd" as an antiracist gesture. Wise argues this phenomenon
explains how whites who harbor stigmas toward African Americans
could wholeheartedly support a black candidate for president. While
Wise acknowledges that Obama's white support is unprecedented, sig-
naling that we have at least moved beyond old-fashioned racism "rooted
in conscious bigotry and hate" (24), he argues that what we are ultimately
witnessing in this historical moment is a shift in white racial consciousness in regards to "exceptional Negroes"; that is, Obama's election shows
that black elites have broken new ground (which is not to say that black
elites are in any way insulated from institutionalized racism or structural
inequalities). As for Black America at large, the longstanding barriers to
social equality and racial justice remain largely intact.

Notwithstanding its "benefits" to Obama's rise to the presidency,
enlightened exceptionalism has been particularly harmful to the black
poor because it trivializes the crippling historical effects of institutionalized racism and structural inequalities on African American self-
determination. As Sut Jhally and Justin Lewis explain in "White Responses: The Emergence of 'Enlightened' Racism," the long-held white
supremacist idea of biological racial determinism, whereby Africans
and African Americans were perceived as naturally inferior to whites,
has been replaced by a cultural determinism that treats blackness as
a kind of curable malady. The thinking goes that a select few African
Americans can overcome this malady and rise to normative (read: white)
levels of social, moral, economic, and intellectual achievement if they
so choose. Jhally and Lewis explain that this new and more insidious
pattern of what they call "enlightened racism" is inextricably tied to late
capitalism and romanticized notions of meritocracy and social mobility
in the United States. On the one hand, enlightened racism still adheres to
the idea, albeit with far more ambivalence than in previous generations,
that whites and blacks are "irrevocably tied to discrete cultures." On the

other hand, it subscribes to the idea that class mobility is possible for ev-
eryone, regardless of their race, class, or creed. A "capricious" and elastic
discourse, racism has "adapted to this discursive climate by absorbing
a number of contradictions" (76). Within this new discourse of racism,
the history of black oppression and white racial exploitation is ensconced
in an "iniquitous capitalist system, where economic rather than racial
laws ensure widespread racial segregation and disadvantage. These, in
turn, encourage white people, looking around them at the compara-
tive prosperity of whites over blacks, to believe in an imagined cultural
superiority and simultaneously to give credence to the idea that we are
only what we become" (76). This mindset is able to thrive in the current
era because the "phenomenon of racism, unlike inequality of wealth and
opportunity, is understood not as a consequence of social structures but
as the collective sum of individual opinions. If white people, as individuals, the thinking goes, stop discriminating against black people, then
racial equality is suddenly possible" (77). In the absence of class analysis,
then, white people are empowered to see African Americans as culturally inferior: "This classless logic says that if most black people fail when
there are no individuals discriminating against them, then there must be
something wrong with them" (77).

The authors argue that blacks like Bill Cosby, Shelby Steele, Thomas
Sowell, and, to a lesser but significant degree, Barack Obama, have as-
similated this mindset, projecting that racial disadvantages are "something that black people are born with rather than something imposed
upon them" (77). Cloaked as liberalism, enlightened racism lets whites
off the hook for white privilege and the various engines of dominant
power that perpetuate structural inequalities. Moreover, it allows them
to embrace black elites, like Cosby and the Obamas, who are "just like
us" without having to answer for their "unstated rejection of the majority
of black people . . . who are not 'like us'" (77).

The problem becomes exacerbated tenfold when "exceptional Negroes" traffic in or embrace their received exceptional status. Exceptional
negro par excellence Bill Cosby is a glaring case in point. Who can forget
his highly publicized rant in 2004 at the NAACP gala event commemorat-
ing the fiftieth anniversary of the *Brown v. Board of Education* decision.
Among his most controversial statements, he uses an analogy of a black

youth getting shot by the police for stealing a pound cake to make a point about self-determination and the problem of blaming whites for black social ills. When the black thief gets "shot in the back of the head over a piece of pound cake," Cosby preaches, "...we all run out and we're outraged, 'Ah, the cops shouldn'ta shot him.' What the hell was he doing with a pound cake in his hand" (online). Cosby aims his barb here at what he perceives as the self-defeating victim mindset among blacks, a mindset that erroneously displaces the blame for intraracial social and economic ills onto whites. More specifically, his explosive analogy conveys that black outrage at police brutality is inherently uncritical and enabling, giving irresponsible and reckless members of the community (who Cosby clearly identifies as the black poor) a "race pass" for criminal behavior that should be unequivocally condemned. Wedded as blacks are to victimization status, they have missed the mark. The problem is not white oppression and racist, trigger-happy policemen, but blacks' wholesale defense of black criminality and irresponsible behavior. The message in short is that slavery and segregation no longer impede black self-determination. To be successful in this new and inclusive racial milieu, blacks need to root out intraracial patterns of self-destruction. Blaming whites and structural forces emerges as self-destructive, giving cultural license to black complacency, slothfulness, and criminal behavior.

In his famous rejoinder to Cosby's argument, *Is Bill Cosby Right?: Or Has the Black Middle Class Lost Its Mind?*, Michael Eric Dyson rightly notes that Cosby plays fast and loose with the institutional structure of entrenched black poverty and criminality. In his speech Cosby posits that individual acts trump institutionalized socioeconomic inequities without regard for the facts and historical precedence. Dyson asserts that "Cosby's position is dangerous because it aggressively ignores white society's responsibility in creating the problems he wants the poor to fix on their own" (182). The fact that Cosby was "enshrined by conservative white critics as a courageous spokesman for the truth that most black leaders leave aside" (182) bespeaks the cultural payoff of enlightened exceptionalism for black elites. Indeed, they are "rewarded" for their indictment against the black poor and uncritical endorsement of self-determination with everything from media commendation to job promotions. Or, as the case was with Cosby, they acquire the cultural capital of being viewed by whites and many black elites as insightful and heroic. Dyson notes there was nothing new or particularly radical about Cosby's call for black personal responsibility and self-determination: "Self-help philosophy is broadly embraced in Black America; but black leaders and thinkers have warned against the dangers of emphasizing self-help without setting it in its proper context. It creates less controversy and resistance—and, in fact, it assures white praise—if black thinkers and leaders make whites feel better by refusing to demand of them the very thing that whites feel those leaders should demand of their followers, including the poor: responsibility" (183).

## ENLIGHTENED EXCEPTIONALISM AS POLITICAL CAPITAL

For his part, Obama tends to leverage enlightened exceptionalism for political gain. As his apologist posture toward Reid, Biden, and others indicate, Obama wants to demonstrate, especially to independent and Democratic white voters, that his is not—nor will it ever be—a racial agenda. In short, he was a new kind of black presidential candidate, not to be confused with the likes of Rev. Jesse Jackson or Al Sharpton. In point of fact, Obama wanted to convey that he was running for the president of the United States not simply Black America. While it is certainly true that Obama's options were limited in terms of how to handle such racial controversies—after all, he wasn't going to become president without appeasing a significant swath of white voters, many of whom fell into this enlightened exceptionalism camp—his calculated choice to become a black apologist for racist language and behavior was ill-advised. Jewish hip hop scholar-critic Adam Mansbach hits the nail on the head to this end in his essay, "The Audacity of Post-Racism." While a strong supporter of Obama for president, Mansbach argues that Obama's "post-race" posture romanticizes lingering structural in-equalities and plays into the hands of white privilege. Mansbach sees the declarations of a post-race society that have accompanied Obama's rise to prominence as dangerous because they suggest that as a nation we are "post-racist." The underlining premise is that blacks can no longer use the "excuse" of racism to explain their social and economic shortcomings. In this white privilege formulation, only blacks are truly post-race. Mansbach expounds that the "essence of white privilege is not knowing you have it; white people are bicyclists riding with the wind at their backs, never realizing that they owe part of their speed—whatever speed that is—to forces beyond their control" (75). He observes that while these forces do not guarantee white success, "few whites are conditioned to contemplate how much worse off they might be if they had to grapple with factors like police profiling and housing discrimination, in addition to the other travails being an American in the twenty-first century" (75). Referencing Obama's famed "race speech," Mansbach argues he consistently let whites off the hook for white privilege by placing white and black experiences of socioeconomic realities on equal footing. To pull this off, Obama had to abandon "the empirical and speak the language of the emotional. Hence, the focus [in the speech] on how people 'feel'—privileged or not, racist or not—rather than on the objective realities of what they have and do and say" (75). While Mansbach acknowledges the tricky balancing act that Obama must perform to appease white voters, he concludes that such appeals to white privilege is ultimately counterproductive, especially as they concern addressing racial inequalities. "Soft-pedaling the reality of white privilege might help bring people to the table, but if they come under false pretenses, they won't stay" (83).

Obama's oft-used phrase of "knowing the hearts" of those whites, within and even beyond his inner Democratic circle, who verbalize racially insensitive or bigoted opinions confirms Mansbach's argument. What Obama communicates via such language is that individuals' words and actions do not represent how they feel or what they believe. This racial logic is "a dramatic reversal of the standard criterion for judgment. Usually, we seek to be judged by our actions, not our thoughts, and we accept that the former are a manifestation of the latter. The success of the [Michael] Richards–[Don] Imus–[Trent] Lott strategy, it would seem, hinges on the fact that it has become more acceptable to spout racism in the public arena than to accuse someone else of spouting racism" (78). Mansbach is accurate here to a point. The caveat we would add is that this formulation holds true for whites only. In the post–Civil Rights era, white claims of "reverse discrimination," how-

ever erroneous or outlandish, garner far more media attention and serious political scrutiny than do legitimate complaints by blacks. Indeed,
a significant number of the population at large view legislation such as
affirmative action as proof that blacks and people of color have unfair
advantages in hiring, college admissions, and the like that are not avail-
able to whites. This thinking is particularly twisted as it concerns affirmative action (which over the last decade has been virtually stripped
of any legal muscle) given that middle-class white women are—and
have been—the chief benefactors of the legislation. Because historical
amnesia and enlightened exceptionalism radically shape racial thinking
in the modern era, the systemic disenfranchisement of African Americans through slavery, Jim Crow segregation, and sharecropping to name
a few, tend to drop out of discussions of blacks' current socioeconomic
position. This explains how, say, legacy college admissions[1] at public and
private universities and colleges, which benefit whites and disadvantages blacks and people of color, fly under the radar of public scrutiny,
while affirmative action, which is a comparatively recent policy and
equally benefits whites is constantly under attack as discriminatory
against whites.

As for this debate over enlightened exceptionalism, it is important to
understand that ultimately words do matter. Regardless of what Obama
may desire, what he says and how he behaves on race matters have direct
impact on the ways that whites see and treat African American communities and social policy. By perpetually steering away from addressing
racism as such, he is essentially bankrupting the term of its political ef-
ficacy, something that blacks generally and the black poor in particular
can ill afford. The famed "Battle Royale" scene in Ralph Ellison's *Invisible
Man* comes immediately to mind as an example of how the language
of race is deeply politicized. The unnamed protagonist of the novel—
an "exceptional Negro youth" and aspiring race leader—has received
an invitation by the local white businessmen and dignitaries to deliver
his valedictorian speech which advocates a Booker T. Washington*esque*
approach to black self determination and personal responsibility. Naïve
to the perverse pageantry of why he was being asked to the deliver the
speech in the first place, the invisible man finds himself lumped in with
another group of black boys who were also invited to the gathering to

participate in a battle royale. Instead of being treated with respect and dignity, the invisible man becomes part of the white spectacle of orchestrated black infighting via the battle royale. By the time the invisible man is asked to give his speech, he has been severely bloodied from the fight—which he loses—and shuffled through a series of cruel hazing rituals designed ostensibly to humiliate and dehumanize. As the invisible man delivers his speech to a raucous white audience, he accidentally says "social equality" instead of "social responsibility" (after the reveling white powerbrokers goad him into repeating the term over and over) when addressing how African Americans need to respond to their socioeconomic circumstances. This apparent slip of the tongue is met with instant rebuke from the audience who respond to his terminology as treasonous. After the invisible man "corrects" himself and accommodates the expectations of his audience, they "reward" him with praise and a full scholarship to attend a historically black college.

To understand how Ellison's satire works in this scene requires an understanding why the word "social equality" is so explosive in this (white) context. One of the strategies of dominant power is to the highjack the language of the oppressed to serve its ideological ends. (A salient white example of this phenomenon in twentieth-century American literature is, of course, John Steinbeck's *Grapes of Wrath,* wherein white working-class union organizers are stigmatized as Communists or "reds" to allow corporate conglomerates to exploit working-class labor.) In the 1950s setting of *Invisible Man,* "social equality" was bound up with a white supremacist ideology, which held that granting blacks equality would put white women in danger of being raped by black men. Indeed, D. W. Griffin's 1915 film *Birth of a Nation* was premised on that very notion. The first American blockbuster, the movie glamorizes the Ku Klux Klan as necessary defenders of white women's virtues against rapist black men. Such thinking explains why a common white retort in the 1950s to explode such arguments for social equality was, "Would you want your daughter to marry one?"[2] The ability to articulate one's experience of oppression was, at bottom, a rather complex and vexing matter. Indeed, one of the oft-ignored psychological burdens of black oppression was proving that one's experiences of oppression were real and not mere "hallucinations,"[3] to borrow Barbara Christian's coinage.

To reiterate a point made in Chapter 1, Barack Obama's rise to the presidency has, in many ways, made it more not less complicated to speak truth to power about the lingering burdens of structural inequalities. Despite the fact that Obama is an exceptional individual across the board in terms of his speaking skills, intellect, poise, leadership abilities, and the like, by virtue of his blackness, his achievements become the de facto measuring stick for what's possible for all blacks regardless of individual circumstances and socioeconomic disadvantages. This phenomenon becomes, to borrow Ralph Ellison's phrasing, the "tricky magic"[4] of normative whiteness. On the whole, Obama's success does not prove that racial barriers no longer exist to black achievement, rather, that exceptional African Americans working exceptionally hard can break through. In truth, Obama has achieved success in spite of racial barriers not in the absence thereof. Obama's appeal to white voters who subscribe to enlightened exceptionalist thinking was precisely his skill at massaging the racial barriers and obstacles of his and other "exceptional" blacks sojourn to the top. William Jelani Cobb states the matter plainly, writing that Obama "was the beneficiary of a vision [of a post-racist America] that we believe in but that does not exist" (20). Referencing Obama's now iconic speech during the Democratic convention in 2004 in which he famously stated, "There is not a Black America or a white America. . . . There is the United States of America," Cobb elaborates,

> Here is what we know of the various Americas on that night in August 2004. Some 21 percent of black men in their twenties were incarcerated, and one third of black children were living in poverty. Hispanics were 3.3 times more likely to be in prison than whites, and their per capita income was 50 percent of their white counterparts. Some 35.9 million Americans—more than 10 percent of the total population—lived below the poverty line, and the quality of public education reflected those disparities. There was not only a Black America and a white America, but a rich one and a poor one, a privileged one and a neglected one, an American where much was possible and one anchored in place by despair. (20)

Cobb points out that Obama was not unlike other past presidential hopefuls, like Franklin D. Roosevelt, to the extent to which he emphasized social ideals over social realities. A key difference, however, is that Obama's idealism pivoted on an American romance narrative of racial unity and equality, a narrative that, while far from being realized in any substantial way in the public domain, reflected what many whites believed was already the case despite data to the contrary. Mansbach suggests that the romance narrative goes further still: many whites feel that they "have been rendered voiceless, that to be black is to be 'lucky.'" From this skewed racial perspective, they perceive whites as the "new racial underclass" (79). He argues that this thinking was the driving force behind Geraldine Ferraro's outlandish claims that Obama owed his success in the Democratic presidential primaries to his race.[5] He opines that Ferraro—a staunch Hillary Clinton supporter and the first woman to appear on a major presidential ticket for vice president—was largely insulated from public indictment because her warped racial notions were largely in line with the "identity frustrations of white youth." Indeed, Ferraro (re)presented herself as a victim of the "race card," arguing that "political correctness" made it impossible for her to speak out about racial matters without being accused of being racist (79).

Cobb comes at the problem of Obama's post-racial rhetoric from a different angle. He notes that accommodating a post-racial stance makes Obama and black politicians in general ineffective leaders on matters pertaining to extant racial inequalities. To support his claim, he uses then–presidential candidate Obama's 2008 response to the fatal shooting of Sean Bell—an unarmed black man who was gunned down by the police on what would have been his wedding day. Rather than express outrage, Obama "called for calm and respect for the law, which struck some as inordinately even-handed in the face of an outrage" (159). Even as Obama's post-racial evenhandedness allowed him to sidestep a potentially explosive issue, it obscured the issue of racial injustice at hand. Cobb writes, "The Achilles' heel of the 'postracial' politician—to the extent that such a thing exists—is that there are consistent, clockwork moments of racial outrage that level-headed appeals for calm simply can't address" (160). The post-racial politician, then, finds him- or herself in a bind, as post-racial politics "was always based on the paradoxical assumption that leadership can exist outside the currents that affect the people that they are leading." Cobb notes there is a subtle but critical distinction between being "above race and beyond it" (160). To extrapolate on Cobb's thinking, to be "above race" is to recognize racism as an ongoing problem even as you navigate an agenda that must prioritize dominant group concerns. In contrast, to be "beyond race" is to create an agenda that treats racism as passé and thus forecloses the possibility of addressing historical wrongs or blazing new paths to opportunity. The pressing question becomes how can one solve a problem that has been (re)presented as no longer existing. In the final analysis, Cobb thinks that Obama—and, indeed, all black politicians who owe their success in large part to black constituencies—have a unique responsibility to address race-group concerns. "At some crucial points Obama would have to behave as the black president, not to the exclusion of his other assignments but surely in addition to them" (161).

The irony here, as Cobb astutely points out (and we expound on in chapter 4), is that the very enlightened exceptionalist thinking that allows whites to view Obama as an exception to the rule of black racial inferiority is also the thinking from within black political and activist circles that lets Obama off the hook for his responsibilities to a "black agenda." Whereas it is common practice across the major parties to take seriously, if not prioritize, the concerns of the constituencies that ushered them into office, many black politicians and activists argue, in fact, that Obama shouldn't be held to a higher standard than any of the preceding white presidents on matters pertaining to race. This appeal to fair treatment flies in the face of racial realities, however. What excited most blacks about having a self-identified black person as president was precisely the fact that such an individual would be able to identify and address the unique circumstances confronting Black America—a luxury that, up to this point in history, had been reserved exclusively for whites. To give Obama a pass on such matters in many ways defeats the purpose of having him in office in the first place. If this line of reasoning appears narrow in racial scope, it is only because white privilege affords whites the luxury of not having to concern themselves about whether the president identifies with their subjectivity as whites. Doing so is an unwritten part of the job requirement. Obama's presidency brought this dynamic out into the open because, as a black man, he had to prove time and again to whites that he was committed to following this unspoken racial script.

Black conservative Shelby Steele's now infamous book, *A Bound Man,* identified this reality of pleasing whites as an albatross that would eventually doom Obama's presidential campaign. Though Steele obviously miscalculated how the election would play out, his insights on Obama's dilemma as what he calls an "Iconic Negro" are nevertheless instructive, especially as they concern enlightened exceptionalism. Steele defines "Iconic Negroes" as high-profile African Americans who have perfected the practice of manipulating white guilt as a means of career success. In Steele's formulation—which is decidedly ahistorical in scope—white guilt is the chief apparatus for blacks in the twenty-first century to attain power, status, and prestige. "Challengers," which Steele clearly disdains, are blacks, like Al Sharpton and Jesse Jackson, who (in Steele's view) approach all whites as guilty until proven innocent on matters of race. To earn racial absolution, whites must prove in some substantial, material way to challengers that they are not racists. While effective to a degree, challengers rarely, if ever, enjoy appeal beyond black spaces. In contrast, "bargainers," the category that Obama, Cosby, and Oprah fall into, are blacks that extend whites the racial largesse of giving them the "benefit of the doubt" when it comes to expectations of racist behavior; that is, they treat whites as innocent until proven guilty on matters of race. So intense is the need to be free of racial guilt, whites express their gratitude to bargainers with jobs, promotions, and fame. Steele refers to Barack Obama as a "rock star" bargainer who "live[s] in that territory between the doubt [he] feel[s] . . . over the self-suppression [he] doe[s] in order to make things happen" for black people "and the charge from [his] own group that [his] success proves [him] be [a] sellout" (91). Steele concludes that challengers and bargainers are doomed to fail because their appeals to white guilt require them to wear racial masks and traffic in victimization.

While Steele's assessment of Obama's racial double bind vis-à-vis whites as a bargainer is problematic on multiple levels (he basically sees Obama as a self-help conservative trapped in a victim-centric liberal political party because of his reliance on victimhood and white guilt) and arguably tells us more about Steele's identity crisis[6] than Obama's, his assertion that Obama is compelled to wear a racial mask to curry favor with whites is compelling, if not undeniable. When Michelle Obama let slip during the campaign trail in Madison, Wisconsin, that "for the first time in my adult lifetime, I am really proud of my country," a collective "amen" emerged from both her immediate audience and the African American public at large ("Michelle Obama: 'For the First Time'"). Moreover, many had a sneaking suspicion she was not only speaking for herself but for her husband as well. If Michelle Obama was a liability at times on the campaign trail it was precisely because hers was not as "perfected" a mask as her husband's. Her frankness on racial matters also paradoxically made her an even bigger hit in the black spaces than Barack.

If Obama is wearing a mask for the sake of political expediency, it stands to reason why—after the political fallout he suffered for defending Henry Louis Gates and discussing extant racism within the police force—he has not only skirted the issue of race but also proactively sought to admonish or silence African Americans individually and collectively, who he perceives as stirring up trouble for his agenda. The most salient target of this move to silence has been Shirley Sherrod, the one-time Georgia state director of rural development for the U.S. Department of Agriculture. Sherrod was forced to resign on July 19, 2010, when Tea Party apologist and blogger Andrew Breitbart posted video excerpts of a speech Sherrod delivered at a NAACP event that same year on his website. The video was released in reaction to the NAACP's accusations of racism against the ultra-conservative Tea Party movement. In the video Sherrod, whose father was murdered with impunity[7] by a white farmer in 1965, appears to admit acting racist toward a white working-class farmer. What the maliciously edited clip does not show, however, was the second part of Sherrod's statement in which she states that, despite how whites had discriminated and terrorized her family over her lifespan, she appealed to the better angels of her character. Not only does she assist the white farmer but goes above and beyond the call of duty and defends him against a shady corporate takeover of his property. When the video went viral and garnered the attention of the national media and press, Sherrod's supervisor, Tom Vilsack, acting under the authority of the White House, fired her without so much as an investigation into the matter or even viewing the video in its entirety. When the truth was finally revealed—which included emotional testimony by the white farmers whose farm Sherrod helped save—Obama extended her an apology over the phone. Tom Vilsack and the White House then later offered her a better paying job within the Office of Advocacy and Outreach, which deals with civil rights areas. Not content to play nice— even with the first black president offering a personal apology—Sherrod turned down the offer and filed a series of lawsuits. Obama and the White House's aggressive move to override termination protocols, if not the law, to fire Sherrod and tamp down a brewing media storm is telling in a very disturbing way about how issues of race are playing out in the Obama administration. It is difficult to imagine that this scenario would have played out the same way had Shirley Sherrod been white and, say, a card-carrying member of the Tea Party.

## IS IT REALLY *JUST* A BLACK THANG?: COLORISM, MERITOCRACY, AND ENLIGHTENED EXCEPTIONALISM

In his iconic satire *Black No More,* George Schuyler's parodies the tenacity of colorism within black spaces. In the novel, a black scientist creates a machine that can transform blacks into whites. Though the scientist charges a steep price for this service, blacks line up in droves to change their racial status. The prominent leaders of the black struggle—most of whom are light skinned and "color-struck"—see this movement as a threat to their livelihoods and try to no avail to derail it. If Schuyler successfully captures the dirty little secret of sustained colorism in black spaces, he underestimates how this phenomenon operates with equal intensity among whites. The novel portrays African Americans as the chief colorists. In truth, colorism emerges out of a white supremacist ideology that maps a wide array of stigmas onto black and brown skin. What Harry Reid's comments about white voters and Obama's light skin simply indicate is that this white supremacist ideological formulation is still alive and potent. We can trace this phenomenon back to U.S. slavery wherein skin complexion and European features played a major role in how enslaved Africans were situated within the slave "hierarchy." Though slavery was, at bottom, a dehumanizing and exploitive experience for enslaved Africans regardless of their skin tone, lighter skin did, in many instances, give those who had it a leg up in slaveocracy over those who did not. Lighter-skinned blacks, in many instances the result of sexual domination by white men over black women, were typically tapped to be house slaves and thus avoided having to work in the fields with the majority of the slaves. More than anything else, however, black light-skin-privilege was used as a wedge to divide and control enslaved Africans. (As Harriet Jacobs clarifies in *Incidents in the Life of a Slave Girl*, being light skinned, particularly for black women, hardly altered the terms of white commoditization and sexual abuse.) While the popular dichotomy between house slaves and field slaves romanticizes the horrors of slavery of which no enslaved group was exempt, what emerged from this practice of favoring lighter-skinned and more Eurocentric appearing blacks over darker-skinned and more Afrocentric ones, was a de facto pecking order of privilege within and beyond white spaces.

However "inartful" were Reid's comments about the benefits of Obama's light skin to appeasing white voters, he was reflecting a measurable reality of colorism that remains intact today. Shankar Vedantam explains that empirical evidence demonstrates that colorism continues to have a major impact on racial realities. He notes that the test-score gap between lighter-skinned blacks and darker-skinned blacks is nearly as large as the test-score gap between blacks and whites. Moreover, "Lighter-skinned Latinos in the United States make $5,000 more on average than darker-skinned Latinos" ("Shades of Prejudice"). What's under attack in the discourse of colorism is not individual blacks so much as "blackness itself." Insofar as colorism's impact on Barack Obama and the white vote, Vedantam cites an experiment during the fall of the 2008 presidential race by Drew Westen, a psychologist at Emory, that sought to measure how much racial complexion figured into white responses. In the experiment whites were shown different ads in support of Obama: "One version showed a light-skinned black family. Another version had the same script, but used a darker-skinned black family. Voters, at an unconscious level, were less inclined to support Mr. Obama after watching the ad featuring the darker-skinned family than were those who watched the ad with the lighter-skinned family" ("Shades of Prejudice"). Intrinsically aware of such internalized racial biases, opponents of Obama ran attack ads linking Obama with defamed politician Kwame Kilpatrick in which Kilpatrick's skin complexion, which is already darker than Obama's, is darkened even further. Vedantam concludes, "Though there can be little doubt that as a candidate Mr. Obama faced voters' conscious and unconscious prejudices, it is simultaneously true that unconscious colorism subtly advantaged him over darker-skinned politicians" ("Shades of Prejudice").

That enlightened exceptionalism is, on some level, tied to skin complexion cannot easily be denied. Barack Obama fit the bill as someone who could realistically compete for the presidency not only because of his temperament, intellect, and rhetorical skill (which is not to say that whites are held to the same standard, as the preceding Bush years dramatically bear out), but also because his skin complexion and Eurocentric features made him more appealing in the eyes of whites. This is a significant qualification because it underscores the variables of racial consciousness that continue to inform our decision making. Indeed, Obama's breakthrough does not necessarily demonstrate that America is *colorblind* as much as it demonstrates that it has advanced to a more nuanced level of *color bias*. It is, in fact, the nation's drive to adapt a colorblind/post-racial approach to discussing racial matters that people of color generally and African Africans particularly must constantly fight against. Riffing on W. E. B. Du Bois famous declaration in *The Souls of Black Folks* that "The problem of the twentieth century is the problem of the colorline" (5), scholar-activist Vijay Prashad writes that the "problem of the twenty-first century is the problem of the colorblind." He expounds,

> This problem is simple: it believes that to redress racism, we need to not consider race in social practice, notably in the sphere of governmental action. The state, we are told, must be *above* race. It must not actively discriminate against people on the basis of race in its actions. At the dawn of a new millennium, there is widespread satisfaction of the progress on the "race problem"; this is so to some extent, but the compass of attacks against blacks and Latinos remains routine. If we do not live by 1896's *Plessy v. Ferguson*, we continue to live by its principle axiom—that "race" is a formal and individual designation and not a historical and social one. That is, we are led to believe that racism is prejudicial behavior of one party against another rather than the coagulation of socioeconomic

injustice against groups. If the state acts without prejudice (that is, if it acts
equally), then that is proof of the end of racism. Unequal socioeconomic conditions of today, based as they are on racisms of the past and of the present, are
thereby rendered untouchable by the state. Color-blind justice privatizes inequality and racism, and it removes itself from the project of redistributive and
anti-racist justice. This is the genteel racism of our new millennium. (38)

To be blind to color and colorism in this context is to license racial injustice and to ignore the historical trajectory of disenfranchis-
ment and exploitation that have landed African Americans and people
of color in a subordinate status position. Enlightened exceptionalism
thus affords whites the luxury of having their racial cake and eating it
too. If racism is conceived as a personal rather than an institutional concern, then, it's not difficult to make the case in the twenty-first century
(especially with a black president residing in the White House) that
government mandates to level the racial playing field are unnecessary,
if not outright biased against whites. When Obama not only skirts such
issues as racism and colorism, but co-signs a similar practice by whites
such as Reid, Biden, Joe Wilson, and the Tea Party, he further trivializes
the unique and underpublicized cost of being black in America. Thomas
M. Shapiro argues that while whites hold a major financial advantage
over blacks because of inherited wealth (a historical product of both
slavery and black disenfranchisement), what sustains this advantage
socially is as important as the actual monetary advantages. He observes
that the bulk of wealth in this country is concentrated among a small
group of whites. Meaning that the majority of whites *do not* inherent significant wealth. "What is really being handed down from generation to
generation is the profound legacy of reproducing racial inequality. The
legacy [is] difficult to discern because the language of family heritage
hides it from our political consciousness" (32). The "language" to which
Shapiro refers is the language of colorblindness/post-racialism. When
we put race back into the equation, we see white privilege at work instead of true meritocracy. In essence, whites have inherited wealth that
was ostensibly generated on the backs of African Americans. What's
passed down through generations is an abdication of responsibility for
this legacy and for the spoils that even working-class whites continue
to reap from it. The situation is akin to finding a bloodied bag of money

at your doorstep every month and spending it freely without seriously questioning where it came from or whose blood has been spilled to make it possible.

When in 1961 Robert F. Kennedy made the bold prediction that there would be a black president in the next thirty or forty years, James Baldwin shot it down instead of praising it. However, it was not the prediction itself that most bothered Baldwin, but the fact that Kennedy's prediction pivoted on the twisted notion that it was blackness, not manufactured barriers to justice and structural inequalities, that blacks would need to overcome to achieve this lofty feat. In *The Fire Next Time* Baldwin writes,

> White Americans find it as difficult as white people elsewhere do to divest themselves of the notion that they are in possession of some intrinsic value that black people need, or want. And this assumption—which, for example, makes the solution to the Negro problem depend on the speed with which Negroes accept and adopt white standards—is revealed in all kinds of striking ways, from Bobby Kennedy's assurance that a Negro can become President in forty years to the unfortunate tone of warm congratulation with which so many liberals address their Negro equals. It is the Negro, of course, who is presumed to have become equal—an achievement that not only proves the comforting fact that perseverance has no color but also overwhelmingly corroborates the white man's sense of his own value. (94–95)

A real "breakthrough" for Baldwin would mean the explosion of this normative white ideology, which already figures blackness as a burden to be overcome rather than an invented barometer of a marginalized groups' subjectivity within normative whiteness. It was for this reason that Baldwin argued that white supremacist ideology was the true (dis)ease of America, a (dis)ease that threatened to contaminate the very core of democracy. Read against Baldwin's formulation, enlightened exceptionalism is just the latest metamorphosis of this racial calculus. Indeed, Baldwin's assessment of how enlightened whites would treat a black president adequately reflects Obama's honeymoon period in the (white) mainstream following the election. That Obama has both embraced and leveraged this proffered "exceptional" status does not bode well for African Americans in the future. If his response does nothing else, it trivializes Black American struggles and the direct role the federal government did—and does—play in them. Regrettably, Baldwin's critique about what electing a black president would mean in America is as relevant now as it was when he wrote it over forty years ago. What remains to be seen is if the "breakthrough" on matters of race that he outlines will be realized any time soon. If Obama's embrace of "exceptional" status is any indicator, we still have quite a ways to go.

# 3

## The Audacity of Reverend Wright

*Speaking Truth to Power*
*in the Twenty-First Century*

He's a politician, I'm a pastor. We speak to two different audiences. And he says what he has to say as a politician. I say what I have to say as a pastor.

—*Rev. Jeremiah Wright*

A civilization is not destroyed by wicked people; it is not necessary that people be wicked but only that they be spineless.

—*The Fire Next Time, James Baldwin*

Although it seems heaven sent, we ain't ready to have a black president

—*"Changes," Tupac Shakur*

IN *THE FIRE NEXT TIME* James Baldwin tackles a thorny political issue of his day concerning how Black America should respond to rising
influence of Malcolm X,[1] Elijah Muhammad and the Nation of Islam
(hereafter NOI). While Baldwin disagrees with their invented religious
doctrine, which casts whites as devils and blacks as God's chosen people,
he nevertheless agrees with many of their assessments of how the dominant culture manipulates power. In particular, he defends Malcolm X's
argument for black self-defense in the face of sanctioned state and federal
violence. In response to Malcolm's assertion that whites expect blacks to

accept levels of subordination that they wouldn't dream of acquiescing to themselves, Baldwin writes, "In the United States, violence and heroism have been synonymous except when it comes to blacks, and the only way to defeat Malcolm's point is to concede it and then ask oneself why this is so" (58). Instead of treating the NOI as a discrete political/religious culture, Baldwin highlights the ways in which the black nationalist group reproduces the white male supremacist ideology that it fiercely attacks. Rather than reject the premise of racial superiority outright, the NOI merely inverts and revises it to serve their own political ends. The "curse of Ham" is replaced by the narrative about mythical white corruption, dating back to the beginning of time. Responding to the "white liberal" assessment of the NOI as morally corrupt, anti-American, and irredeemably racist, Baldwin opines that what these "white liberals" hate about how the NOI expresses its will to power is precisely what it defends to the death about the right of white dominance over all other non-white groups in the United States. Baldwin notes that the NOI's contrived religious narrative about whiteness and devilry is no more or less fanciful and insidious than the biblical account of the "curse of Ham" that whites used to justify slavery and the Jim Crow era of segregation that followed. Contrary to what liberal whites might like to believe, what they were witnessing in the NOI was a reflection of their own domination theology. Not one to be pigeonholed into established modes of thinking, Baldwin writes that he refuses

> to be put in the position of denying the truth of Malcolm's statements [about the U.S's double standards on race, violence, and heroism] simply because I disagree with his conclusions, or in order to pacify the liberal conscience. Things are as bad as the Muslims say they are—in fact, they are worse, and the Muslims do not help matters—but there is no reason that black men should be expected to be more patient, more forbearing, more farseeing than whites; indeed, quite the contrary. The real reason that non-violence is considered to be a virtue in Negroes . . . is that white men do not want their lives, their self-image, or their property threatened. (59)

Baldwin punctuates his assessment of whites' double standard on black revolutionary action versus white revolutionary action when he notes the mindset of the African American Christian that "defected" to the NOI as being profoundly logical. Given their subordinate and dehumanizing experiences of discrimination in the country at the time, blacks didn't need the NOI or any other black organization to sell them on the idea that "whites were devils." If anything, the NOI provided blacks with something they had suspected all along, "that they had been lied to for all these years and generations, and that their captivity was ending, for God was black" (50). It is not difficult to see in this instance how one person's radical anti-Americanism was another person's righteous and revolutionary uprising. The point was not to determine which group, the NOI or liberal whites, were at fault so much as to point out how white power and hegemony dictates not just the terms of the racial debate but also the terms of reality itself.

We invoke Baldwin's iconic critique *The Fire Next Time* as a critical backdrop to think about why Obama's relationship with Rev. Jeremiah Wright and activist black church Trinity United played out in the media and within black spaces in the ways that it did. Following Baldwin's example of investigating the metadiscourses that inform the versions of racial realities that are legitimized and dismissed, this chapter demonstrates how the impulses to defend white privilege and deny ongoing racial inequities sparked the media scapegoating of activist black churches in general and Rev. Wright and Trinity United in particular. We use the term "activist" black churches to register the myriad cultural, theological, and political diversity of black religious institutions. This is a crucial distinction, as the idea of a unified black church continues to resonate in the public domain and political rhetoric even as the immense diversity in denominations, theology, culture, politics, and outreach is on full display. Indeed, as Barbara Dianne Savage notes in *Your Spirits Walk Beside Us,* "Despite common usage, there is no such thing as the 'black church'" (9). Moreover, explains Savage, the idea of black churches as inherently activist flies in the face of history. These received notions of church as a positive political force grow out of a revisionist historical impulse, wherein the black religious involvement in the Civil Rights Movement (which, in reality, was significantly fractured and uneven) has become the basis on which many historians, cultural critics, and others use to think about African American religious organizations across time. The concentrated black religious participation in the Civil Rights

Movement (and there certainly were many institutions that either remained silent or even denounced the protests) was a historical aberration
rather than business as usual in black religious spaces. The consequence,
however, of such concentrated religious participation has fueled a revisionist history of sorts that colors over the significant tensions among
the personal, political, and religious in manifold black church communities. Savage writes, "Black religious belief and black religious life, by
their very nature, are resistant to external reach and control, including
from those who seek to harness their powers for a collective purpose on
behalf of the race as a whole" (8). Historically speaking, black religious
institutions have hindered as much as helped antiracist political cam-
paigns, even during the celebrated Civil Rights era.

If these misconceptions are prevalent in how the nation thinks about
African American history, they were also prevalent in the ways that the
mainstream media (mis)represented Reverend Wright, Trinity United,
and the activist elements within segments of the black religious tradition. Conspicuously absent in the media coverage concerning the activist arm of black religious institutions was any serious engagements
with the white supremacist elements within mainstream Christianity
that pressed blacks to strike out on their own and, in some instances,
to develop black nationalist approaches to practicing Christianity. The
institutionalized historical amnesia on race relations in the country all
but assured that Reverend Wright and Trinity United would be tagged
as un-American and racist in the media. Pushing against this political
current, we argue that Wright's propensity to "act up" in the pulpit and
speak truth to power as it concerns struggling black communities (even
if, at times, his claims are more conjectural than factual) is an asset rather
than an obstacle to African American empowerment in the twenty-first
century. Given that the public face of the "black church" tends to be that
of black megachurch leaders like T. D. Jakes, Eddie Long, and Creflo
Dollar who subscribe to largely apolitical, prosperity-centered ministries, it becomes imperative for African Americans who see black religious institutions as useful political entities to stand up against mischaracterizations of activist black church organizations and leaders. While
African Americans are certainly not the only ones that should take up
this responsibility—for surely there are whites that see, understand, and

have a crucial stake in these politics as well—the reality is that if blacks do not speak out, the mischaracterizations will gain traction and shut down a important medium through which African Americans challenge institutionalized white supremacy and structural inequalities.

That Obama was an active member of Trinity United and once a great admirer of Reverend Wright's activist-intellectual approach to community uplift would seem to be a cause for optimism rather than alarm. However, as we will show, Obama's political shift in step with the political demands of getting elected has set a dangerous precedent, especially as that shift allowed post-racialists across political lines to (re) present activist black churches—which exist, in large part, to counteract the insidious social, economic, and emotional legacy of white oppression—as hostile, militant, anti-white, and anti-American institutions. While it is certainly true that Obama was pressed into distancing himself from Wright and Trinity United as a practical means of political survival, most cultural critics and political pundits have dramatically minimized or conveniently glossed over Obama's agency in this process, particularly as it concerns how he let whites off the hook for extant racial injustice and structural inequalities in his famed "race speech." The problem is that many critics view Obama's successful political negotiation of the Wright controversy as a victory for Black America. Obama maintained his poise under fire and turned what could have been a death knell for his campaign into a political bonanza. The "enemy" emerges in this cultural scenario as the mostly white constituencies within and beyond the Democratic Party that sought to bring down Obama. Reverend Wright emerges, at best, as an unfortunate casualty of (white) media spin and, at worst, as an arrogant and prideful old-school preacher who allowed whites to use him as a pawn to vilify Obama. As good politics go, Obama's handling of this white-hot controversy was noteworthy. But as the de facto representative of Black America (a role he has frequently used to his political advantage), his handling of events covered over the lingering effects of institutionalized white supremacy on black socioeconomic realities.

This chapter investigates how such post-racial posturing affects activist black church organizations and progressive religious leaders, like Wright, who speak their minds about extant racial inequalities without concern over political fallout. Tellingly, very few media outlets ventured to seriously engage Wright's claims about racism and federal-sanctioned terrorism and human rights violations. In truth, most African Americans—even some who had intimate knowledge of Wright's social contributions and the truth of his racial claims—were so anxious to see Obama succeed that the consequences of Obama's ultimate denouncement of Wright and Trinity United were either dismissed as insignificant or outright ignored. While the cultural impulse to support Obama is certainly understandable given the torrid history of denying African Americans access to higher office, the besmirching of Wright, Trinity United, and the activist black church tradition should not be taken lightly, especially in African American spaces. Even though Obama's opponents did not win the battle, so to speak, in derailing his presidential aspirations, they certainly won the ideological war in dictating the terms of black protest in the twenty-first century. This outcome was certainly not a given. Theoretically speaking, had the likes of T. D. Jakes, Creflo Dollar, or Eddie Long thrown their support behind Wright, the outcome would have most certainly been different. The conspicuous silence from these and other prominent ministers speaks volumes about what is tragically wrong with apolitical and prosperity-driven ministries. It also shows why Jeremiah Wright and his ilk—like civil rights religious titans who preceded them—will always be on the outside looking in when it comes to getting a full hearing in the (white) mainstream. Wright's true transgression in the public domain was not that he lied about the federal government's involvement in terrorist activities, illegal wars, and experiments on Black America or, for that matter, that he intentionally provided Obama's opponents with political ammunition, but, rather, that he articulated an inconvenient (racial) truth and refused to be silent or even to soften his message. Indeed, for a significant portion of Obama's black supporters, Wright's defiance was nothing short of racial treason. The nation's first serious black presidential candidate was on the brink of capturing the Democratic nomination and possibly the White House and rather than step out of the spotlight after clips from his fiery sermons started to circulate in the media, Wright chose to fight back and defend his legitimate claims. While Obama is fond of situating his historical achievements via the Civil Rights legacy of Martin Luther King Jr., the reality is that in sticking to his guns on racial matters and not caving to pressures within and beyond black spaces to pipe down, it was Wright, not Obama, who most reflected the radical Civil Rights leader's political stance.

## REVEREND WRIGHT AND THE INCONVENIENT TRUTH

> The government gives them the drugs, builds bigger prisons, passes a three-strike law and then wants us to sing "God Bless America." No, no, no, God damn America, that's in the Bible for killing innocent people. God damn America for treating our citizens as less than human. God damn America for as long as she acts like she is God and she is supreme.
>
> —*Rev. Jeremiah Wright, sermon in 2003*

> And the code [of U.S. politics] says that you're either supposed to lie, as long as the lies are generally accepted, or talk about vague things like America's greatness or the audacity of hope. But never, never talk about things that are true and that matter.
>
> —*David R. Henderson, "Jeremiah Wright: True and False"*

In *The Substance of Hope* William Jelani Cobb provides a useful glimpse into how Black America responded to the Reverend Wright political controversy during a critical stretch in Obama's Democratic presidential campaign. As most will recall, the controversy erupted when sound bites from several of Wright's most fiery sermons, including a jeremiad in which he blames perpetual U.S. government corruption for sparking 9/11, began to circulate in the media. Not surprisingly, the media played up the most provocative aspects of the sermon, particularly Wright's assertion that the nation's illegal wars and human rights violations helped spark 9/11. The clear political goal of the media campaign, hatched in large part from constituencies on the far right, was to bring down Obama's campaign. Hillary Clinton, who at the time was lagging in the poles, seized the opportunity of the moment and began to pound away at the Wright/Obama association. The media blast set Obama's campaign on its heels and put his presidential aspirations in serious jeopardy. As Obama's success among white voters hinged in large part on his "exceptional Negro" status and avoiding the tag of "angry black man," the Wright controversy was particularly explosive. Adding fuel to the fire was the fact that Obama had lauded Wright time and again in books and speeches as the man that inspired him to become a Christian and a vocal champion for the weak and dispossessed. Indeed, Obama's named his second and bestselling book, *Audacity of Hope,* after a Wright sermon. What Obama couldn't afford politically—at least as far as whites were concerned—was being associated with racial anger embodied in Wright's rhetoric. Though by this point in his campaign Obama's popularity among blacks was skyrocketing, his was still a developing political brand, and he couldn't rest on his political laurels, especially given that many blacks could—and did—empathize with Wright. Obama passed this political test with flying colors by delivering his famed "race speech," which cleared the way for Wright, characterized as a shortsighted relic of a bygone racial era, to make a graceful exit from the public spotlight.

Rather than accept the received terms of his public silencing, Wright reignited the political controversy in an interview with Bill Moyers and shortly thereafter in a televised speech at the National Press Club. When asked to respond to Obama's handling of race on the campaign trail, Wright asserted flatly that Obama is "a politician, I'm a pastor. We speak to two different audiences. And he says what he has to say as a politician. I say what I have to say as a pastor. But they're two different worlds" ("Transcript," online). Though stated without malice, Wright was clearly expressing his dissatisfaction with Obama's unflattering portrait. The tag "politician" in Wright's comments was transparently pejorative, suggesting that Obama was being less than truthful in his speech, that he was throwing his pastor "under the bus" and soft-peddling the reality of racism to appeal to white independents and Democrats. Moreover, Wright's speech at the National Press Club was clearly delivered as a "signifying" response to Obama's race speech. Though Wright's message is also about racial unification and striving for democratic harmony, he focuses on the racial inequalities that continue to preclude the kind of post-racial reality that Obama's speech framed as a fait accompli. He also argues passionately that blacks have—and continue to be—the targets of racial discrimination despite claims in the media and beyond that the country is moving toward a more inclusive climate. In a clear rebuke of Obama's lofty rhetoric of racial reconciliation, Wright asserts, "I come from a religious tradition that does not divorce the world we live in from the world we are heading to. I come from a religious tradition that does not separate the kingdom of heaven that we pray for from the devious kingdoms of humans that keep people in bondage on earth" ("Transcript," online).

Colorblindness for Wright is not the path to racial reconciliation but a way to pathologize (black) racial difference, trivialize the disparities of power, and erase the harsh realities of being black in America. In his speech Wright reiterates that "difference does not mean deficient" ("Transcript," online). His intent was to shine light on the ways that the discourse of difference generally and white supremacy more specifically have been used by those with power to denigrate and exploit those without. Wright's thinly veiled point was that however inspiring we might find Obama's post-racialist rhetoric, he is projecting a vision of what might become of race relations, not the reality of how they currently stand. If Obama casts himself in his race speech as a referee for all things racial and resists "taking sides," Wright casts himself on the side of Black America and particularly the black poor. Though Wright's black nationalist thinking is not without its flaws—he essentializes blackness and reinforces the gross misconception of Africa as a monolithic culture[2]—he underscores a series of inconvenient truths, including the fact that whiteness continues to be the measuring stick of normalcy and achievement in the United States, while blackness, in contrast, continues to function as the mark of deviance and lack. (As noted earlier, blacks like Obama, Oprah, and Cosby are perceived in the public domain as "honorary whites"—that is, blacks who have managed to "transcend" race/blackness and rise to the level of white achievement.)

Cobb represents one of a cadre of notable African American figures that view Wright's speech and his choice to "talk back" to the media as a big mistake. Cobb characterizes Wright as arrogant, naïve, and politically out of step with the enormity of the historical moment. He writes, "Black preachers are afforded a phenomenal degree of power. Spending years in front of an audience that literally says amen to your opinions often leads to an attendant degree of self-import and narcissism and a low threshold for criticism" (33). Making matters worse, Cobb argues, Wright was not sufficiently media savvy:

> It must have been unspeakably difficult for Wright to see his work and reputa-
> tion be defamed for weeks on end, but he entered the press conference with
> a flawed agenda: The commercial media do not specialize in reconciliation.
> Wright dismissed Obama's words as political rhetoric and defended his
> "Goddamn America" statements. But the content was nearly irrelevant; what
> mattered was the way those words would be consumed, filtered, repackaged and
> distributed. He was like a man who has lost a hundred dollars to a card hustler
> and believes he can break even by playing again. (35)

While Cobb does well here to explain why Wright ultimately failed in his attempts to tamp down the controversy and clear his name, he rehearses a rather unoriginal and deeply problematic assessment of Wright's significance in this political theatre. Even if Wright is arrogant and self-centered in the ways that Cobb describes (accusations, consequently, that have also been levied against Obama by his opponents), it does not necessarily follow that his assessment of extant racism and structural inequalities in the country is wholly inaccurate. Nor, for that matter, does his anger at how blacks have been (mis)treated mean he is a lunatic or his anger is unjustified. It was none other than white conservative, Hoover Institute scholar David R. Henderson who put it best on this score in a 2008 op-ed, "Jeremiah Wright: True and False":

> Many of the conservative commentators have claimed that Wright's speech was
> full of hate. Now, it's possible that Wright hates people, but all I could see clearly
> from reading or listening to his [National Press Club] speech is that it was full
> of anger. Anger does not equal hate. They can go together, but they don't have
> to. Indeed, I've found that the more clearly I've expressed my anger, the less hate
> I've had. (online)

Henderson rightly argues that anger properly channeled is not only useful but healthy—presenting a pathway beyond hatred. What even Henderson sees in his fact-finding analysis of Wright's most controversial claims is that the overwhelming majority of them are true. Contrary to media spin, Wright was on target with his condemnation of how the federal government abuses power and mistreats its African American citizens. If Wright was angry, then, as his critics accused, he had plenty of cause to be.

We must also reconsider the (unsubstantiated) argument that Wright was shortsighted in his belief that whites would not ultimately vote for a black man for president. For argument's sake, if it is indeed true that Wright miscalculated the significance of the political moment and the new reality that whites would, in fact, vote for a black man for president, it was a "logical" miscalculation, not one borne of being out of step with how blacks are fairing in late capitalism and in the social sphere. As Cobb rightly notes, history is notoriously "lopsided," meaning that the unpredictable happens all the time. In this case, the United States was prepared to elect a black man (that identified as such culturally) *despite* the lingering racial stigmas about blackness and structural inequalities that continue to dog Black America. Though Wright's skepticism about what was possible racially in the twenty-first century proved ultimately to be wrong, the skepticism itself was certainly justified given the patterns of white responses to Black America to date. As the media also pivots on enlightened exceptionalist thinking, which means that pathology-centric models of blackness and black masculinity in particular still reign supreme, we must be careful to distinguish between the lived reality of blackness versus the media-spun reality of blackness. Wright is a lot of things, but a crazed, anti-American lunatic he is not.

Obery M. Hendricks Jr.'s essay "A More Perfect (High-Tech) Lynching: Obama, the Press, and Jeremiah Wright" offers perhaps the most insightful critique of how someone of Wright's high social standing and respect in both black and white spaces became the target of media (mis) information. Most notable about Hendricks's position is that he focuses on how Wright's life and the activist black church were grossly mischaracterized and outright slandered in the public sphere. Hendricks starts his essay by invoking the heinous lynching of Sam Hose in April 1899 in Georgia and explaining how the white-controlled media turned a clear-cut act of self-defense[3] into a premeditated murder. An educated, upstanding, and law-abiding citizen, Hose was recast in the media as a cold-blooded murderer and rapist of a white woman. Hendricks argues that what made Sam Hose's act of self-defense so threatening to the white status quo was that it challenged the premise of white supremacist ideology at its core. In shooting a white man even in self-defense, Hose was exerting his agency to defy white inhumanity and institutionalized black subordination. Hose was made an "example of" in both the brutally ritualistic way that white mobs lynched, tortured, burned, and severed his body and in the ways that the media "lynched" his character in the press. The public spectacles that were Hose's body and media lynching served notice to African American communities that the facts of such an incident were secondary, if not inconsequential, to the larger political goal of maintaining the white status quo of supremacy. Hendricks draws a direct line from Hose to Wright, noting that both media "lynchings" were fueled by a similar desire to defend white privilege and distort the historical realities of racial oppression. Riffing on Clarence Thomas's twisted victim appeals during his heated Supreme Court Senate confirmation hearing in which he characterizes his opponents as performing a "high-tech lynching," Hendricks argues that the real high-tech lynching occurred to Reverend Wright.

Countering Cobb's portrait of Wright as arrogant and out of touch, Hendricks offers a portrait of Wright as a man who is humble, insightful, intellectual, inclusive, and generous to a fault. Hendricks not only calls our attention to Wright's laudable record of community involvement and military service but highlights how the mainstream media ignored or drowned out the critical mass of whites who jumped to Wright's defense. Of particular note in this regard are white clergy within the United Churches of Christ denomination who uniformly praised Wright's community service, theology, and racial inclusiveness and defended the much-maligned (and now removed) statement on Trinity United's website describing the congregation as "unashamedly black." (The United Churches of Christ happens to be a predominantly white denomination with a rich history of antiracist agitation—a history that was a direct catalyst for Wright's decision to join their ministry.) It was indeed renowned white religious historian Martin E. Marty who shed light on the media spin of the statement as racist. He rightly observed that being "unashamedly black" is not the equivalent of being "anti-white" (Hendricks, 166). Race pride in this context is a useful, if not necessary, coping mechanism to offset the legacy of slavery and Jim Crow segregation.

In *The Preacher and the Politician* Clarence E. Walker and Gregory D. Smithers explain why such statements of black racial pride bother post-racialists whites:

> A large part of the answer to [why whites were so threatened by Wright] rests on acknowledging that the black Christianity that Wright and millions of other African Americans practice decenters whiteness as normative in Christian identity and religious practice. Whiteness as the norm is at the core of modern definitions of "postracialism" and "color blindness," and those espousing these notions therefore deem assertive, self-respecting, proud blackness to be extremely threatening to social cohesion in the United States. Indeed, in historical and contemporary terms, all forms of black nationalists—be they black Christian nationalists, Muslims, Afrocentrists, or black secularists—insist that the people they represent must be liberated from the psychological domination of whiteness, or, in modern parlance, "postracialism." (35)

In other words, being "unashamedly black" is a cultural defense posture against the devastation of institutionalized and government-sanctioned white supremacy. To focus as the media did on Trinity United's race pride is to distort the reality of blacks' assertion of agency in a hostile and intensely raced U.S. environment. In a wicked sleight of hand, the historical victimizers and beneficiaries of institutionalized racism and white privilege succeeded in blaming their defiant victims for having the gall to fight back and exert black pride. Such hypocrisy would be laughable were it not for the real and deleterious consequences that such ideological blind spots have on social policy, the judicial system, education, crime prevention measures, and the like. Wright and Trinity United are certainly not laughing. Wright's unimpeachable record as a community activist and defender of the dispossessed has been sullied beyond repair. Not only has he received numerous death threats—the emotional toll of which is difficult to measure—but he has suffered financially as well. A highly sought-after speaker prior to the Obama debacle (a primary source of his income), Wright now struggles to find work.[4] Suffice it to say, social pariahs are not exactly in high demand as speakers. Concomitantly, the Trinity United congregation is now synonymous in the cultural lexicon with radical (read racist and anti-American) black churches. While it is difficult to measure how much this stigma will impact the congregation going forward, one thing is certain. They are taking heat for precisely the type of self-determination and community-building efforts that Obama and even many conservatives identify as crucial to turning things around in hard hit and impoverished areas.

These post-racial blind spots also explain why a couple of Wright's less credible stances on racism—like the argument that the U.S. government created HIV/AIDS—received such uncritical analysis in the media. As Hendricks asserts, it was hardly an accident that the media focused narrowly on the veracity of such claims rather than the climate of corruption and white medical malfeasance that rendered them conceivable to so many African Americans. Regarding the HIV/AIDS conspiracy argument, Hendricks asserts, "Wright's suspicions (about state licensed medical experimentation of black bodies) were not farfetched. Indeed, there is incontrovertible evidence that on numerous occasions officials at the local, state, and federal levels of government have subjected black people to clandestine medical experimentation and outright abuse," including the egregious Tuskegee Experiment wherein over four hundred black men were intentionally used as lab rats by Public Health Service physicians. With little regard for black humanity, the doctors manipulated the men into believing they were being treated for syphilis when, in fact, they were being given a placebo. As untreated syphilis can lead to blindness and brain damage, the white physicians literally watched as the black men collapsed into madness and irreparable physical decay. Walker and Smithers put an even finer point on the debate, noting that conspiracy theories are commonplace among historical oppressed groups—"such as the Armenians who were slaughtered by the Ottoman Turks or the Jews killed by the Nazis" (28)—that have a history of being targeted and abused by local, state, and federal powers: "Since medical experimentation on black people is part of the black American historical memory, it is glib and insensitive to dismiss Wright as a crank and conspiracy theorist for making similar claims" (29). Walker and Smithers further note that it was none other than Michelle Obama who put a stop to a papillomavirus medical experiment on black girls that was put forth in 2001 by the University of Chicago Medical Center when she was serving there as a vice president of community affairs. Her reasoning for putting a stop to the experiment grew directly out of her historical memory of the Tuskegee syphilis experiment and other such white experimentation on black bodies.[5]

White blindness and Wright's conspiracy theory aside, Hendricks's otherwise insightful essay takes a political turn that underscores why it is so difficult within and beyond black spaces to discuss the Wright/Obama controversy in terms of culpability. Hendricks vacillates between condemning Obama for taking the easy way out of the controversy by embracing a version of the conservative right's (mis)characterization of Wright as politically out of touch and holding the media and the political right fully responsible for putting Obama in an untenable position that forced him to "diss" Wright and the activist black church. Hendricks charges, "Even though Obama knew that Wright spewed no hate and no anti-American sentiments, in the end, he disowned who Wright is and what he stands for." In the very next sentence, Hendricks asserts that Obama's race speech "is the speech of a politically astute man who had been placed in the unenviable position of contributing to the ruination of the reputation of a man he deeply admired, but who seemed to have no other choice if he could make a positive difference for all Americans. It was a choice he should have never had to make. It is to the shame of America that he had been forced to" (178).

While there is no debating that Obama was placed into a difficult spot, he made a conscious and, indeed, calculated *political* decision to cast Wright as a cultural relic even though, as Hendricks rightly notes, Obama never contradicts any of Wright's claims in his speech. The point here is simply this. Despite being "blacker than an episode of Soul Train," to adopt Cobb's description of Obama, he is nevertheless an ambitious, seasoned, and shrewd politician who understands all too well that accommodating the (racial) status quo—not fighting it—is the path to social acceptance. In other words, while Obama is clearly a principled man, he is obviously not beyond doing what politicians do when confronted with a controversy of this magnitude. In a word, Obama cut his losses. Though to his credit, Obama did not denounce Wright outright in his speech, as many of his supporters had hoped, he did "disown" Wright, to borrow Hendricks language, which, in our estimation and certainly Wright's, is hardly a consolation prize. As Hendricks rightly notes, there were significant consequences for Obama's actions. Chief among them he helped participate in Wright's high-tech lynching; put "a paradigm in place for discrediting and destroying any influential black minister who raises a critique of the abiding racism in America"; made an "example" of Wright in the media, deterring any future black ministers from going down the same path; and, finally, he has implicitly declared "that African American ministers, no matter how well informed, will not be allowed to engage in serious public debate about government policy without repercussions, unless their stated positions support the status quo" (182).

Even though Wright had his supporters (black and white), they didn't constitute a critical mass and thus couldn't presumably muster up the necessary pushback to offer a corrective to the widespread misinformation about Wright's character and achievements. This dynamic begs the question: What role did Black America play in Wright's public smearing? It is hardly speculative to say that the majority of Black America cheered on Obama's handling of the Wright controversy even as perhaps most agreed in principle with the preacher's characterization of extant racism in America. As many blacks, especially those in high-profile fields, are often thrust into the unsavory position of having to bite their collective tongues about racism in the workplace to appease whites and remain employed, there was probably more than a little empathy for Obama's (white) predicament. Moreover, it is still the case that many African American's subscribe to a kind of black messiah leadership thinking. Such a leader is typically male, commands the respect or serious attention of powerful whites, and tends to be either deeply religious or a minister outright (think Frederick Douglass, Booker T. Washington, Marcus Garvey, Elijah Muhammad, Malcolm X, Martin Luther King Jr., and, more recently, Jesse Jackson Sr., Al Sharpton, and Louis Farrakhan). What sets Obama apart from these other leaders is crossover appeal. It is no accident that African Americans began to rally around Obama when he pulled off that stunning upset in Iowa—one of the whitest states in the nation—during the Democratic presidential primaries. This is not to say that African Americans blindly supported Obama because he was black. Indeed, history demonstrates that whites, not blacks, are the most racially biased voters. As Cobb reminds us in *The Substance of Hope,* blacks have been voting for whites for as long we have had the right to vote. Whites, on the other hand, have only recently come around to voting for non-white candidates. It was, in fact, Obama's uncanny ability to speak across racial lines—to speak about sensitive racial matters that would typically send whites running for the hills—that captivated Black America.

As the popular Obama T-shirts featuring him alongside antislavery and Civil Rights titans like Frederick Douglass, Malcolm X, and Martin Luther King Jr. dramatically attest, Obama was viewed by a significant portion of Black America as the next major black Civil Rights leader. In many ways this black messiah complex and climate of celebration explain why black communities brushed off Reverend Wright's high-tech lynching so easily. The striking paradox concerning African Americans and racism is that despite the gory history of white oppression in the United States, African Americans remain hopeful—though certainly not to the extent as whites—that our country will eventually live up to its promises of equality and equal opportunities. The skyrocketing level of optimism about racial progress that immediately followed Obama's election (and which has dropped off since even as his approval rating remains high) throws this reality radically into focus. In short, Wright was up against more than simply Obama's opponents; he was pushing against the headwinds of a tornadic swell of black enthusiasm and support. Wright didn't have a fighting chance of survival.

While it is far too early to write the obituary of the activist black church tradition, Wright and Trinity United's high-tech lynching certainly raises the question: What role is there for activist black churches to play in this so-called post-racial era of politics? Worth pointing out here is that activist black churches of Trinity United's ilk are woefully in the minority in terms of visibility, financial resources, and media clout compared to the black prosperity-ministry driven megachurches. A key barometer of just how powerful and resourceful these black megachurches have become was witnessed recently when Eddie Long—an outspoken opponent of gay marriage—made headlines for allegedly coercing several young men in his congregation into sex. Located in Atlanta, Georgia, Long's New Birth Missionary Baptist Church has a membership that exceeds 25,000. His yearly compensation is in excess of three million dollars, which includes the use of a $350,000 Bentley automobile. In terms of Long's political reach, four presidents (George H. W. Bush, George W. Bush, Jimmy Carter, and Bill Clinton) and then-senator Barack Obama attended New Birth when he officiated Coretta Scott King's funeral. Of all the pressing issues in Black America (like the prison industrial complex, judicial injustice, and hiring discrimination), Long has thrown his considerable political might and resources behind fighting against gay marriage and women's rights to abortion. Leaving aside the obvious irony of Long's alleged sexual misconduct with young men, what we see in his choice to champion policies that deny civil rights to women and gays is the political bankruptcy of such prosperity-gospel-driven ministries.

In *Watch This!: The Ethics and Aesthetics of Black Televangelism,* Jonathan L. Walton usefully contextualizes the problematic microsocial politics of prosperity-gospel-driven megachurches. Walton premises his critique on Peter Paris's theory of "priestly" and "prophetic" black preachers. In Paris's theory, priestly black preachers see society as "fundamentally good and attribute injustice to the moral indiscretions of a few as opposed to inherent flaws in the structure of society" (Walton, 211). They place emphasis, then, on integrating their parishioners into the status quo rather than on challenging the structure of the society: "By nurturing humility, patience, and goodwill, priests accommodate themselves to social injustice without necessarily affirming it. In other words, priests at most encourage microsocial resistance among their parishioners by helping them endure those things that cannot be readily changed" (211). The idea is to help parishioners productively cope with bondage rather than fight against it. As far as social status is concerned, priestly black leaders command the respect of the black masses as well as powerful whites. Operating within the ideological perimeters of "racial common sense" they believe that "they can appeal to the moral goodwill of the societal elite to obtain justice" (211). In this role as mediator between the folk and societal elite, the priestly leaders always seek compromise over conflict, even when the societal elites make decisions that are clearly wrongheaded. Born out of fear, the rationale is that stirring up trouble will make matters worse and greatly compromise the social capital of the leadership.

Prophetic leaders, on the other hand, are social reformers. Their perspective on society is that it is neither good nor bad, but "fundamentally flawed." Their politico-religious activism is driven by their notion of what a just and equitable society should look like. They see their spiritual charge as reforming society toward this perceived social ideal and believe that if they fail to do so society will collapse into destruction: "For the prophet there is little compromise on the tenets of justice and no moral middle ground" (212). What this ultimately means is that prophetic leaders (think Martin Luther King Jr., Fannie Lou Hamer, Malcolm X, and Ida B. Wells) have "no permanent allies or enemies," as their aim of achieving justice and equality for all overrides any social, political, or cultural loyalties.

Walton notes that many African American religious leaders like Long, Jakes, and Dollar identify as prophetic leaders when, in reality, their ministerial patterns are more in line with the priestly leadership model: "Their uncritical embrace of America's social structures—most obviously America's capitalist economy—and the dominant society's morals and manners reflects the nonconflictual approach of the priestly type more than the progressive posture of the prophet" (212). Even though Long and Jakes are inherently political figures to the degree to which they speak out on political issues, including white supremacy, their theological stress on moral behavior as the path to resolving black social woes is "microsocial at best." Walton asserts further that

> political positions that are in line with the majority of Americans cannot necessarily be considered progressive or resistant. Thus antigay marches or protest for prayer in schools, though political, should not be considered prophetic. Bishop Eddie Long, like Elder Michaux and Prophet Jones in previous generations, is the contemporary manifestation of a long tradition of political advocacy dictated by the climate of public consent. Supporting war on the heels of 9/11 or opposing gay marriage while operating in a conservative evangelical tradition does not necessarily call for moral courage or oppositional conviction. If anything, it represents a worldview and activity that almost everyone in the subculture would be comfortable with. (212)

While these "safe" microsocial political measures keep controversy at bay in megachurches, which, in turn, keeps pews and church coffers full, they can have significant impact on how local, state, and federal powers treat important African American social issues. Walton explains that this evasive political posture makes black priestly leaders especially susceptible to becoming complicit in silencing black agitation and protest.

> Black clergy's social mediations between elites and the masses can easily deteriorate into the paternalistic "gift" exchange that has defined the awkward relations between black and white evangelicals for centuries. In the world of contemporary religious broadcasting, rather than receiving building materials or protection for one's church building from white supremacists, prominent African American televangelists are receiving large honoraria, free airtime and exposure on TBN, and faith-based funding from the White House. One could justifiably argue that these gifts are in exchange for black televangelists' resounding silence around issues of social injustice that negatively affect the African American community, like the 2000 and 2004 presidential election fiascos and the federal government's failure to respond to hurricane victims on the Gulf Coast. While these are just two examples, the real danger is when the priestly class trade away social justice for white benevolence—an unfair exchange indeed. (213)

Having a black man in the White House does little to change this raced political calculus, for Obama is directly answerable to the largely white Democratic power structure that embraced his candidacy[6] and largely bankrolled his campaign. Indeed, Obama's political philosophy reflects the accommodationist impulse of priestly leadership. This dynamic is visible in the ways that Obama and his team of handlers pieced together an inspiring narrative of American exceptionalism shot through with (romanticized) Civil Rights imagery that enjoyed broad appeal across racial lines. Thomas J. Sugrue observes that as Obama's political ambitions grew, he distanced himself from the black politicians and historical legacies that made his presidential run a possibility to begin with. Instead of rejecting completely the legacies of Civil Rights, he rejected the aspects of it—namely, the Black Power Movement—that most whites find unsettling. Concomitantly, he "embraced a particular version [of the Civil Rights Movement] . . . that allowed him to synthesize his own identification with the Southern Movement with his political ambition" (48). The problem was that Obama could not "risk association with either [of the Civil Rights Movement's] most principled or its most problematic practitioners, for even though whites professed color blindness, they remained skeptical of politicians whose rhetoric or style appear 'too black' (48). Obama navigated this tension successfully by "aligning himself with the history of the Southern branch of the civil rights movement [that] was safe. The freedom struggle, once divisive, had become domesticated, transformed into a narrative of unity (49)."

Like the priestly black leaders, Obama's message to Black America is that the United States is a fundamentally good and just society. While racial barriers to success still remain, they are few and far between. In short, the major battles for racial equality have already taken place. Moreover, the nation is moving steadily toward its democratic ideals. African Americans should thus be forward thinking as well, concentrating on the immense opportunities for success at their feet, rather than fixating on racial wounds of the past. The chief goal, in fact, should be to seek common ground with one's opponents rather than to concentrate on differences and points of tension. Obama underscored this message in rather dramatic fashion after he became president by picking Rev. Rick Warren to deliver his inauguration invocation. A prominent, white social conservative who backed a California ballot measure banning same-sex marriage, Warren seemed an unlikely candidate for such a high honor, particularly given Obama's strong gay voter support and the way white evangelical leaders, like John Hagee, dogged him throughout the presidential campaign. While Obama cast his choice of Warren as an olive branch to right-wing evangelicals and to highlight Democrats as a pro-Christian party as well, he was also clearly trying to create as much distance between himself and the radical black religious tradition that caused him so much grief during the election.

Though Obama has mostly taken the Black Christian community's support for granted while aggressively going after young, white conservative evangelicals in initiatives like the Joshua Generation Project, he has strategically cultivated relationships with highly visible and respected religious leaders in Black America like Al Sharpton and Cornel West. (Consequently, West has recently fallen out of favor with the president for taking issue with the White House's conspicuous inattention to the struggling black poor throughout his presidency.) This calculated political move is by no means original. Keeping the folks most likely to raise a ruckus in black spaces within arm's reach is a tried-and-true presidential strategy, dating back a half century. This means, in essence, that Obama is following in the footsteps of white presidents who sought to use black leaders to keep the disgruntled black masses in check. And from the looks of Obama's approval rating in Black America (which is holding steady at nearly 90 percent), the strategy has been wildly successful. The only major problem is that Obama cannot seem to motivate blacks to vote in large numbers when his name is not on the ballot, a variable that proved critical in gubernatorial losses in Virginia and New Jersey and in the "shellacking" that the Democrats experienced in the midterm elections.

In many ways, then, the prosperity-gospel-driven megachurches— all of which have ministries and programs that seek to help struggling black communities—are doing their black parishioners a grave disservice. Not only are they letting Obama and elected officials off the hook for ignoring the hardest hit Americans during and after the recession, but they are also sowing the seeds of inaction and accommodationism. The foundational idea that self-determination and moral living alone are the keys to social and economic prosperity is both ahistorical and out of step with socioeconomic realities. This is a particularly dangerous mindset too—even for middle-class African Americans—because it overdetermines individual agency and encourages blacks to look beyond race for answers to their social, cultural, and emotional struggles and for keys to success and prosperity. The problem with this transcendent thinking is, of course, that in a radically raced society the variable of race informs individual and collective behavior even when it's not center stage in the public discussion. This reality becomes clear when considering the hyper-consumerist "bling" mindset that many of these megachurch black leaders embody—if not outright endorse—a mindset that, when boiled down, resembles a similar version on display in commercial hip hop culture. As Walton reminds us in Watch This, African Americans have been classically conditioned to seek the material trappings of the white elite. However, because of slavery, Jim Crow, and a host of institutionalized variables that fostered a significant gap between generational white wealth and black wealth, uncritical black pursuits of a perceived middle-class lifestyle can be fraught with peril. Part of the attraction of many of these megachurch ministers for many African Americans has to do with the way they embody and enact a version of the American Dream. The rags-to-riches rhetoric that is often a staple of these ministers' sermons projects the false notion that it is possible for anybody—with the right moral compass and ambition—to achieve fame and success on the scale of their black clergy. This message is reinforced by the visible trappings of wealth and opulence constantly on display in the ministers' lifestyle. For instance, Long, Jakes, and Dollar wear expensive clothes, live in luxurious houses, drive expensive cars, and fraternize with celebrities. Walton notes that by "promot[ing] the gilded values of conspicuous consumption and hypermaterialism among persons already in fragile financial circumstances," black-prosperity-gospel ministers set up many of their parishioners to fail. This is especially pertinent given the fact that middle-class blacks tend already to invest far more than their white counterparts in depreciable goods like clothing and cars—a pattern that becomes a crucial roadblock to building generational wealth. The irony of the Horatio Algeresque rhetoric that undergirds the messages of many of these prosperity gospel ministers is that it trivializes the fact that their success as entrepreneurs is directly tied to hard-fought civil rights struggle.

## "I DON'T FEEL NO WAYS TIRED": TAPPING INTO THE SPIRIT OF BLACK PROTEST

> Will words become deeds that meet needs?
>
> —Rev. Dr. Joseph Lowery, speaking at Coretta Scott King's funeral in Bishop Eddie Long's church

When civil rights icon Rev. Dr. Joseph Lowery uttered this rhetorical question at Coretta Scott King's funeral, the audience exploded in agreement. The jab, of course, was aimed at sitting president George W. Bush, who was a guest of honor along with three other presidents in attendance. Lowery's comments stood in sharp contrast to that of Long's, who steered clear of politics and treated Bush's attendance as an honor rather than an affront to King's civil rights advocacy. The enthusiasm and respect for Lowery's prophetic rhetoric was in full display. As Bush noticeably squirmed in his seat, Lowery continued his assault to thun-

derous applause, stating that there were "no weapons of mass destruction over there [in Iraq] . . . that there are weapons of misdirection right
down here. Millions without health insurance, poverty abounds, for war
billions more, but no more for the poor" ("Comments at Corretta Scott's
Funeral"). The response to Lowery at Long's church is noteworthy here
because it demonstrates, among other things, that the political bent of a
minister is not necessarily in line with those of his congregants. While
many black megachurch leaders, like Long and Jakes, allowed themselves to be wooed by the Bush White House, African American voting patterns have remained consistent, going back to the Reagan era.[7]
What this demonstrates, on one level, is that African Americans do not
blindly follow the political thinking of their spiritual leaders. That African Americans are making this distinction shows they are acutely aware
that their social fate is determined not just by their moral character,
ambition, and hard work but also by longstanding power structures that
remain tilted in favor of whites.

As for Lowery, he took a lot of heat for his comments. Bush Sr. characterized what he called the "political shots at the president"—which
clearly included Lowery's remarks and those made from President Jimmy
Carter—"as kind of ugly frankly" (online). Bush went on to say, "Anybody that shoots at the president of the United States at a funeral, I just
didn't appreciate that" (Collins). Lowery responded unapologetically
that "at a black funeral we always celebrate the life of the deceased and
take up the causes that the decedent championed. Mrs. King's cause was
peace and racial justice, and I challenged the living to do likewise" (Harris). In a related interview on the *Hannity and Colmes* show, Lowery again
came under attack. Host Sean Hannity accused him of using the funeral
to score political points. The objective of such an event, Hannity argued,
was to honor King's life and legacy not play partisan politics. Speaking
out of the prophetic black leadership tradition, Lowery explained that
by calling Bush out for his crimes against humanity and black people, he
*was* honoring the legacy of Martin and Coretta Scott King. To Hannity's
criticism that his comments were made at an inappropriate time and
place, Lowery countered, "When we started the bus boycott in Montgomery, it was not the appropriate time. When we went to Birmingham
to fight segregation and public accommodations and brutal oppression

on the part of the police department, the preachers said to Martin, it's not the appropriate time" ("Rev. Joseph Lowery Defends His Remarks," online). Lowery made clear that the idea of there being an "appropriate" time to protest only served the interests of those in power. Invoking Martin Luther King's famous letter from a Birmingham jail, Lowery conveyed that breaking the rules of power, not following them, was the key to attaining black civil rights.

If Lowery's speech angered Republicans, it also must have angered Bishop Eddie Long, because he stressed, as did Maya Angelou, that Coretta Scott King championed the civil right causes of straight and gay citizens. Given Long's aforementioned crusade against gay marriage, the comments would have neither been lost on him or his congregation. (As a footnote, outspoken civil rights leader and actor Harry Belafonte was disinvited at the last minute by the King family—a move allegedly engineered by King's daughter Bernice, who is a minister at New Birth— when President Bush decided to attend.) As Lowery's was a prepared speech, his decision to raise the issue of King's stance on gay rights at New Birth was no accident. He knew exactly what he was saying and exactly *where* he was saying it. Suffice it to say, he didn't arrive at the funeral to make friends or to be politically correct. He remained true to his moral principles, meaning in this case that no one, including New Birth and Bishop Eddie Long, was going to be spared his criticism.

Bush's plummeting approval rating combined with a lack of high social interest in the Coretta Scott King funeral largely insulated Reverend Lowery from a concentrated attack. Except for a few verbal dustups with conservative journalists, he emerged from this short-lived controversy virtually unscathed. Indeed, he was tapped by Obama several years later to deliver the Inauguration Benediction. Though Reverend Wright's response to his high-tech lynching grew out of the same prophetic impulse that prompted Reverend Lowery to "call out" Bush, Long, and New Birth at Coretta Scott King's funeral, he picked the wrong time to say the "wright stuff," to borrow Derrick Z. Jackson's phrasing.[8] It was the "wrong time" because—then as now—our country is a nation of cowards when it comes to racial issues, unwilling to confront that which we care not to know about our ugly history. Turning Wright into a scapegoat didn't require a lot of imagination because the social script for doing so has been in place for many years. Martin Luther King Jr. and Malcolm X faced a similar high-tech lynching in their day even though much of those histories have been sanitized and whitewashed. As Reverend Lowery rightly observes, "Dead men make such convenient heroes. They cannot rise up to challenge the images we mold and fashion for them. Besides, it's easier to build a monument than a movement" ("Rev. Joseph Lowery Defends His Remarks," online). Diehard prophetic leader that he is, we doubt Reverend Wright would have changed much about the way he handled the trumped-up controversy. Keep in mind that Wright told Obama a year before he became president, "If you get elected, November 5th I'm coming after you, because you'll be representing a government whose policies grind under people" ("'Coming After You!': Wright Vows to Hold Obama Accountable If Elected"). Considering how close they were at the time and Obama's familiarity with Wright's prophetic leadership style, it's hard to imagine Obama was surprised or offended by Wright's assertion. It's also hard to imagine that Obama didn't take the man at his word. The cold irony here for Black America is it has been prophetic leaders, like Reverend Wright and Reverend Lowery, not politicians, who have typically been on the frontlines in the fight for African American civil rights. Fifty years from now we may look back on this historical moment and realize we allowed ourselves to be snookered: that we should have heeded Wright's advice and treated Obama as the politician he is rather than as the civil rights leader so many wrongly imagine him to be. Only time will tell.

# 4

## Setting the Record Straight

*Why Barack Obama and America*
*Cannot Afford to Ignore a Black Agenda*

But the hushing of the criticism of honest opponents is a dangerous thing. It leads
some of the best of the critics to unfortunate silence and paralysis of effort, and
others to burst into speech so passionately and intemperately as to lose listeners.
Honest and earnest criticism from those whose interests are most nearly touched,—
criticism of writers by readers, of government by those governed, of leaders by those
led,—this is the soul of democracy and the safeguard of modern society.

—*W. E. B. Du Bois, "Of Mr. Booker T. Washington and Others"*

Hope is irrational.

—*Huey Freeman on Aaron McGruder's* Boondocks

WIELDING HIS CUSTOMARY take-no-prisoners satirical approach in his
highly controversial *Boondocks* cartoon series, Aaron McGruder takes
aim at the irrational exuberance that swept over black communities during Barack Obama's historic ascendance to the presidency. More specifically, he uses the *Boondocks* episode, titled "It's a Black President, Huey
Freeman," to underscore the shortsightedness and dangers of conflating
Obama's mainstream political campaign (which perpetually sidestepped
the issues of race, racism, and poverty to court white voters) with the
cultural tradition of radical African American leadership. In the scene,
Huey Freeman, the young outspoken Black Nationalist intellectual,

finds himself at the center of public controversy when the mainstream media tries to link him politically to Obama by virtue of Huey's appearing on Obama's Facebook "Friends List." Invoking Obama's reaction during the Democratic primaries to being linked with the controversial Black Nationalist figure, Louis Farrakhan, McGruder has Obama in the cartoon publically "denounce" and "repudiate" his relationship with Huey. For his part, Huey, whom the mainstream media erroneously tags a radical terrorist for his black nationalist political leanings, stays out of the political fray, electing instead to express his discontent with Obama's racial strategy and African Americans' willful acquiescence to it in nonverbal displays of disgust. Indeed, though Huey never openly attacks Obama's racial politics, McGruder conveys them visually in the large iconic portrait of Malcolm X on display on Huey's wall as a German reporter interviews him about his lack of enthusiasm. The portrait of Malcolm X conveys to the viewer that Obama—for all of the praise that he receives within Black America as a great leader along the trajectory of Martin Luther King Jr., Malcolm X, Rosa Parks, and others—is hardly radical. Nor, for that matter, is he willing as King, Malcolm, and Parks were, to risk life and limb to speak truth to power concerning blacks' extant subordinate social and economic status. As the German reporter probes Huey for some modicum of excitement over the historical election of Barack Obama, he finally asks the question: "What is wrong with letting people be happy? Can too much hope possibly be a bad thing?" Huey replies flatly, "Hope is irrational." Robert Freeman, Huey's grandfather, exemplifies this "irrational hope" when he states that the black "struggle [for social and economic equality] is officially over" (*Boondocks*).

The black-on-black riot that erupts in the park because Huey responds to an enthusiastic Obama supporter's rhetorical question of "aren't you excited?" about the prospects of having a black president with an unenthusiastic "eh" is a brilliant comedic moment. Laid bare are the ways in which the meteoric black support for Barack Obama's presidency prevented much-needed scrutiny about what his racial agenda as president would mean for Black America and, more specifically, for the black poor. Ostracized from mainstream Black America (and even from his own grandfather, who publicly denounces him), Huey is hilariously reduced to teaming up with the self-hating, racial outcast, Uncle Ruckus, if only because he needs a ride to Canada and no one else with a driver's license will talk to him. The episode ends with Black America suffering from a collective hangover, resulting from the realization, several years into Obama's presidency, that his status as president has meant little to nothing in terms of how blacks are treated and viewed by the federal government and the dominant culture at large.

## THE COST OF BLACK CONSENT

As outlandish as McGruder's representations of blacks' enthusiasm and support for Obama might first appear, in many ways it accurately reflects the cultural variables and pressures that dictated how blacks responded individually and collectively to his candidacy. More specifically, the episode forecasts the dangers of blacks' unbound, wholesale investment in Obama's presidency. To wit, Huey's radical stance against the tide of enthusiasm within Black America for Obama during the election bespeaks the reality that Obama's agenda is hardly "black," radical, or even politically progressive.

We open this chapter with this controversial *Boondocks* episode because it brilliantly contextualizes the political blind spots in Black America toward Obama and his post-racial political agenda. As several black prominent and outspoken Obama critics have discovered, criticizing the nation's first black president—however legitimate or respectfully delivered that criticism may be—comes at a very high price. Consider the string of African American attacks leveled at Tavis Smiley—a wildly popular black syndicated radio and talk show host—when he became an outspoken critic of Obama during the presidential election. What makes Smiley such a beloved celebrity in Black America is his consistent championing of black causes, particularly those that seek to improve the lives of the black poor. Not one to shirk from controversy, Smiley has been a lightning rod at times for taking unpopular stances, from criticizing the racially insensitive language of white rapper Eminem to taking civil rights leaders, like Jesse Jackson Sr. and Al Sharpton, to task for various political missteps. Indeed, he prides himself on keeping the dream of Martin Luther King Jr. alive by giving a voice to the poor and challenging the claims, intent, and actions of politicians that represent Black America. Among his portfolio of successful media interest is his annual hosting of the State of the Black Union, where race-conscious leaders, ranging from Louis Farrakhan and Cornel West to Hillary Clinton and Mae Jemison, debate the politics of being black in America and strategize for a better future.

Feeling that he had established enough goodwill among Black Americans to speak freely, Smiley took an aggressive approach to Obama during his run to the presidency, challenging him on various fronts to clarify how he would address black concerns as commander in chief. Though he began to take the most heat for his stances within Black America when it became evident that Obama could actually win the presidential race, Smiley remained steadfast in his insistence that Obama be held to the same standard of scrutiny as Hillary Clinton, John McCain, and the other white candidates in the race. What he clearly underestimated was how deep and intense the black devotion to Obama would become. Though Smiley always made a point in his criticism of Obama to separate his respect and admiration for Obama *the man* from his expectations of Obama as *the president*, his criticism amounted to "Uncle Tomism" for a major block of his black audience who, as Cobb, Sugrue, and others note, inexplicably viewed Obama as the second coming of Martin Luther King Jr. As Obama's stock in Black American skyrocketed, Smiley's stock began a precipitous fall. In short order, Smiley was dismissed by even his most loyal followers as an Obama-hater (he now shares that dubious distinction with Cornel West and Harry Belafonte). Despite this dismissal, Smiley did not back down. He took Obama to task for what he interpreted as a slight for rejecting an invitation to participate in his State of the Black Union forum—an invitation, consequently, that Hillary Clinton accepted. He was also critical of Obama for not attending the fortieth anniversary ceremony of Dr. King's assassination in Memphis, Tennessee, as well as Obama's decision to distance himself from the controversial Rev. Jeremiah Wright. The public backlash against Smiley in Black America reached a boiling point in 2008, prompting him to announce his resignation as a political commentator on the highly popular *Tom Joyner Morning Show*. Although Smiley initially cited his reason for leaving as fatigue from a busy schedule, Tom Joyner later revealed that the real reason for Smiley's resignation was the backlash he experienced because of his criticism of Barack Obama as a presidential candidate:

> "He called me yesterday and said, 'I quit,'" Joyner said on the air. "He can't take the hate he's taking over this whole Barack Obama thing. People are really upset with him. He's always busting Barack Obama's chops. They call. They e-mail. They joke. They threaten. You know Tavis like I do. He needs to feel loved. We're so emotional about this Barack Obama candidacy. If you don't say anything for Barack Obama, you're considered to be a hater.... It's just that it hurts so deep when the people you love don't agree with you. He loves Black America and Black America has been very critical of him. It hurts. It hurt me to hear Black Americans criticize him." ("Tavis Smiley Quits Tom Joyner Show," online)

Some days later, Smiley rejected Joyner's accounts, reiterating that his resignation had nothing to do with the backlash from his criticism of Obama. While we certainly need to take Smiley at his word, it is difficult to imagine that Joyner's comments are without merit. (Joyner has subsequently sided with Smiley's detractors and attacked his long-time friend as an Obama-hater and sell-out for his poor people's tour with Cornel West and his persistent criticism of Obama's policies toward the black poor in the media.) Never in Smiley's long career had he faced anything remotely close to the kinds of vitriol from within Black America that his admittedly legitimate criticism provoked. This controversy, in fact, continues to dog Smiley to this day. Addressing this controversy in his book *Accountable: Making America as Good as Its Promise* (2009), Smiley writes,

> During the run-up to the 2008 presidential election, while I was still the resident political commentator on the *Tom Joyner Morning Show*, I caused quite a stir among the listeners—who are largely African American—by insisting that we hold then-Senator Barack Obama accountable for his political record and his campaign promises. I wasn't singling him out, but rather applying the same standard to him that we should apply to all. I feel now, as I did then, that it is our responsibility as engaged citizens to expect now-President Obama to live up to the promises that made him an appealing candidate. I want Barack Obama to be a great president. I believe he can be. But, only if we make him a great president by being the kind of active citizens democracy demands. (Smiley and Robinson, xii)

If Smiley's intent in the book was to put the controversy to rest— making it clear that his criticism against Obama was political, not personal—it failed dramatically. As the *Boondocks* episode makes clear,

Black America's support for Obama has reached a fever pitch, and even temperate, critical approaches are often met with resistance. Quite frankly, Smiley didn't stand a chance.

*Huffington Post* political analyst Earl Ofari Hutchinson characterized the black attacks against Smiley as "a verbal public lynching." Addressing the need for such critical engagements with Obama and other black politicians from within black spaces, Hutchinson writes:

> Given the history of the racial scorn heaped on them, blacks should be the absolute last ones to impose a racial code of conduct on other blacks. Unfortunately, in their absolute dogmatic, unyielding, Obama mania, they have turned what in any other season would be a healthy give and take reasoned dialogue and even debate on political issues into finger pointing, name calling, bashing, and yes as Smiley unhappily said "hate" toward any black who disagrees that Obama is the second coming of Dr. King. (Hutchinson, online)

Conflating Obama with King is problematic on several fronts, especially considering the enormous difference in loyalties between a national politician and a civil rights activist. Given how the radicalism of King's activism has been written out of contemporary history (ironically enough, McGruder's *Boondocks* also deals fearlessly with this phenomenon), it is difficult to fully appreciate why this Obama/King conflation is so problematic. The problems of this conflation become clear when we consider the ways in which King bucked the government—at local, state, and federal levels—even at times when conceding ground on several points could have garnered more political capital from powerful white men, including the president. It was, indeed, King's dogged refusal to compromise his moral agenda even at the cost of life, limb, and political capital and his uncanny ability to excite the black masses to action that made him public enemy number one for the federal government and the white elite. On October 10, 1963, Attorney General Robert F. Kennedy authorized the FBI to begin tapping King's phones. After King's speech at the March on Washington, the surveillance officer for the FBI reported to J. Edgar Hoover, "We must mark [King] now if we have not done so before as the most dangerous Negro of the future in this Nation" (Richardson, online).

Invested as he was in his moral mandate, King not only riled the white power elite but also many of his powerful black supporters. The problem for King in the promotion of a black agenda in the 1960s was that it meant a radical critique of white America's moral conduct—a critique that spared no one, including whites who agreed with parts of King's agenda. Many black activists saw King's aggressive critique as overreaching, lumping in would-be white allies with blatant white racists. Sticking to his political guns, King refused to make such distinctions among whites. His uncompromising stance toward an "empathic" white clergy in the now iconic "Letter from a Birmingham Jail" is but one of many instances of this impulse to hold even such well-intentioned whites accountable. King also refused to hold his tongue about his problems with President Johnson's escalation of the Vietnam War and our country's political misdeeds abroad. Some black leaders found this particular stance ill advised, especially as it came on the heels of the president signing the landmark Civil Rights and Voting Rights Acts (Miah, online). During his 1967 speech "Beyond Vietnam—A Time to Break the Silence" at Riverside Baptist Church in New York City, King exclaimed that America is "the greatest purveyor of violence in the world today" (King, online). He also asserted that a "nation that continues year after year to spend more money on military defense than on programs of social uplift is approaching spiritual death" (online). William Jelani Cobb puts the matter succinctly when he writes that had King "been a politician, he would have given Lyndon Johnson his loyalty (or at least owed him a political debt) for signing the Civil and Voting Rights acts. Instead, Dr. King criticized LBJ for escalating the nation's involvement in Vietnam. King retained his moral currency, but his criticism depressed his political stock" (162–163).

As a national politician whose career rises and falls on popular opinion and polling, Obama—unlike King and other civil rights activists— cannot afford to be truly radical. Suffice it to say that if Obama were as heroically impolitic as King, he would not have garnered the resources and political support within his party to capture the presidency, let along the Democratic presidential nomination. To be clear, the point is not that Black America should expect Obama to respond as a no-holds-barred black civil rights activist. But, to reiterate Smiley's point, Black America should treat Obama as the politician that he is rather than the activist for a black agenda that they may desire him to be. In other words, African

Americans need to make Obama earn and work for their vote, not offer it up freely without any expectations attached.

King stoked political controversy as a civil rights activist in order to call attention to the needs of the poor. Obama, as a national politician, calculates each move to maximize political gain and remain in power. Hypothetically speaking, then, even if Obama personally felt that focusing on fighting poverty was ultimately the right thing to do, he would not spend political capital on that endeavor if doing so would put his candidacy in jeopardy. His move to the right after the 2010 midterm elections in which Republicans took control of the House and greatly improved their number in the Senate is a striking case in point. Had the Republicans not recaptured the House and wrested political momentum from the Democrats, Obama would certainly be less accommodating to the GOP, Tea Partiers, and center-right independent voters. Surely, there was nothing radical about extending Bush tax cuts for the rich and reneging on one of his signature campaign promises. What this move demonstrates beyond a shadow of doubt is that Obama is a typical politician and wants, above all, to be a two-term president. Bill Clinton (who Obama tapped to help sell his Bush tax cuts compromise) is a more appropriate comparison to Obama in terms of his political and historical trajectory. In truth, the gulf between Barack Obama, the national politician, and Martin Luther King Jr., the civil rights activist, is quite wide. As we will discuss momentarily, getting Black America to make the distinction is an altogether separate and very daunting and complex matter.

## THE TAVIS SMILEY FACTOR AND SETTING THE RECORD STRAIGHT ON OBAMA AND THE BLACK AGENDA

Not surprisingly, Tavis Smiley was on the forefront of initiating a public debate within Black American about Obama's lack of a black agenda—a debate that sadly collapsed into the finger pointing, scapegoating, and name calling that Hutchinson addresses in his op-ed column. The controversy escalated when Smiley took several prominent black leaders to task on the *Tom Joyner Morning Show* for letting Obama off the hook for not establishing a black agenda. He blasted:

Some of us who call ourselves black leaders are making the wrong choice and I'm afraid this morning Tom that in so doing we are misleading, misguiding black folk. It is time for a course correction, not now, but right now, because leadership without followership is a sinking ship. . . . Over the past few weeks, choruses of black leaders have started singing a new song. I must have missed that choir rehearsal, because I don't know the words to this new hymn, the president doesn't need a black agenda, they sing. He is not the president of Black America, he is president of all America, and he need not focus specifically on the unique challenges Black America is facing, they sing. As you probably deducted by now, I'm having some trouble learning my part and carrying that new tune." (*Tom Joyner Morning Show*, Feb. 23, 2010)

Smiley identified this accommodating "chorus" of black leaders as civil rights leader Rev. Al Sharpton, Harvard University law professor Charles Olgetree, NAACP president Benjamin Jealous, National Urban League president Marc Morial, Obama advisor Valerie Jarrett, and civil rights legend Dorothy Height. He concluded by issuing a call for these leaders to debate or defend their views on Obama's responsibility (or lack thereof) to Black America in a televised forum in Chicago that he was scheduled to host.

When Al Sharpton, who hosts his own show, caught wind of Smiley's comments, he went on the defensive, accusing Smiley of misrepresenting his viewpoint. The public debate intensified further when Smiley called into the show (which also happened to feature Charles Olgetree) to clarify his admittedly scathing indictment of Sharpton, Olgetree, and other black leaders' complicity in giving Obama a free pass on establishing a black agenda. After Smiley came on the air and asked, by way of greeting, how Sharpton was doing, Sharpton snapped back, "I was fine until you started messing with me this morning, what's wrong with you!" (*The Al Sharpton Show*, online). Aware that Sharpton's hostility stemmed from his political commentary on *The Tom Joyner Morning Show*, Smiley responded,

Nothing is wrong with me and I'm not messin with you or brother Olgetree. . . . What I said this morning was . . . on national radio, which I'll say now, is that, we need to have a conversation about whether or not there needs to be a black agenda. And, when there are certain African American leaders . . . , including respectfully and lovely, as I said this morning, the two on this phone right now, who are quoted in the *New York Times* and other places coming out of a meeting in the White House suggesting publicly in the media and to black people that

> this president does not need have an African American agenda, what I said this
> morning . . . [on *The Tom Joyner Radio Show*] and I prefaced it by saying we need
> to come together to have a conversation about what that means, but when black
> leaders start saying to black people and the black media that we don't need to
> have this president focus on an African American agenda given that black people
> are getting crushed. . . . I said we need to come together to have a conversation
> about what that means. I think that there is a disconnection between those kinds
> of quotes and black people. (*The Al Sharpton Show*, online)

Cutting Smiley off, Sharpton responded that the "disconnect" was
not between black leaders' vested interests in supporting Obama at all
costs and championing the needs of the black poor even if doing so
meant calling the first black president on the carpet for being unre-
sponsive to the needs of Black America. Rather, the "disconnect" was
between Smiley, the *New York Times* article in question, and the truth.
Moving from the political to the personal, Sharpton accused Smiley
of blatant disrespect and duplicity. From Sharpton's point of view, this
issue was a "private matter" that should have been handled over the
phone instead of over the airwaves. He fired, "Don't talk to us like we're
stupid, Tavis! . . . If you want to deal with truth, let's deal with truth,
lovingly, but don't love me and distort me [over the airwaves]!" Later,
after returning from a brief commercial break, Sharpton continued his
rebuke:

> I think that the forum that Mr. Smiley is talking about [to discuss Obama and
> the black agenda] should be held by somebody objective, now. I mean you can't
> attack the president for three years like he has, and then turn around and distort
> what civil right leaders are saying, and then you say, I'm going to have the heal-
> ing meeting and I love you no matter what, when you have injured people. I
> think we need to talk about all of these things. (*The Al Sharpton Show*, online)

In the *New York Times* article that sparked this fiery debate, Sharpton is quoted as saying he didn't think Obama should ballyhoo "a black
agenda," and Ogletree remarks that he "finds puzzling the idea that a
president who happens to be black has to focus on black issues." Moreover, longtime civil rights activist Dr. Dorothy Height is quoted, "We
have never sat down and said to the 43 other [white] presidents: 'How
does it feel to be a Caucasian? How do you feel as a white president? Tell
me what it means to you.'" She concludes, "I am not one to think that he
[Obama] should do more for his people than for other people. I want him

to be free to be himself." On the other side of the debate are the Kirwan Institute for the Study of Race and Ethnicity, a coalition of scholars that engages race-related issues and politics and prolific scholar Michael Eric Dyson. (Inexplicably, Princeton professor Cornel West, who has been one of the most outspoken black critics of Obama's inattentiveness to public policy as it concerns Black America, was not cited in the article.) After examining Obama's State of the Union Address in 2010, the Kirwan Institute put out a statement, warning that "continued failure to engage race would be devastating" (Stolberg, online). Michael Eric Dyson is described as "exasperated" by Obama's treatment of black concerns and quoted as saying, "All these teachable moments . . . but the professor refuses to come to class." Dyson's "teachable moment" reference is, of course, a swipe at Obama's infamous "beer summit" (discussed in chapter 1), in which he inserts himself into the Gates/Crowley controversy and addresses racial profiling in policing only to backpedal when faced with a national white backlash. Dyson's point is that Obama, the purported race relations guru, has much to learn about how to address racial problems.

Regrettably, this important debate about Obama and a black agenda never seriously got off the ground. Smiley tried to get one started, but the transparently personal nature of his gripe with the president for skipping out on the State of the Black Union debates (which he mentioned so many times publicly that it became a running joke in black spaces) and his method of "calling out" black leaders for giving Obama a pass on establishing a black agenda severely weakened his credibility and moral authority among his black followers. In truth, while these factors certainly obscured Smiley's critique, they were not the chief reasons his popularity plummeted. The fact is that the quickest way to pariah status in Black America these days is to openly attack the president. However shortsighted were Sharpton, Olgetree, and Height's perspectives on Obama and a black agenda, they had (virtually) the full backing of Black America. If Smiley was guilty of anything, it was of bringing a knife to a gunfight. What Smiley clearly communicated on *The Tom Joyner Morning Show* was that a host of black civil rights leaders, like Sharpton and Ogletree, were compromising Black America, particularly the black working class and poor, by falling in line with the Obama's post-racial philosophy regarding the black agenda. It was a bold move, indeed, considering Obama's popularity in Black America. If Joyner's assessment of Smiley's mindset is accurate, then, Smiley assumed he could press the issue of Obama's inattention to black concerns without taking a serious hit in popularity among his black supporters, the bulk of his listening and viewing audience. The pressing issue is not, of course, defending Smiley's reputation. (To his credit, Smiley has stuck by his guns on this issue, despite the tuning out of his otherwise supportive black audience when it comes to his views on Obama and the black agenda.) The pressing issue is how does Smiley, or any leader or constituency for that matter, help Black America to see that pressing for a black agenda does not necessarily hurt Obama or constitute an act of cultural betrayal—that the bigger risk is to be compliant and hope for the best. Marcia Dyson states the matter plainly in her op-ed "Take Me to the Waters":

> The argument that publicly criticizing our first black president is an act of racial disloyalty is immature. We must be grown enough to know that politics at its best is about engaged citizenship, not tribal worship. You can love black people and do what's best for the race without agreeing with everything the president does or says. If we don't use our public platforms to encourage, solicit and push the president to do what we think is right, we've surrendered both our civic duty and our racial responsibility. (online)

The political pushback by other groups that have been overwhelming in support of Obama, including gay rights groups and Hispanic organizations, demonstrates why it is in Black America's best interest to hold Obama accountable and press him to pursue a black agenda. As president, Obama has been careful to identify with his most highly visible constituent groups: he put forth an agenda to remove the "Don't Ask, Don't Tell" law for gays in the U.S. military, reversed his position on the Defense of Marriage Act stating that his administration would no longer enforce the law, committed the U.S. Attorney General's Office to challenge the aggressive Arizona law allowing law enforcement to stop and search perceived illegal immigrants, took a tough stance on reducing carbon emissions through a climate change bill (to the liking of environmental advocacy groups), and restarted peace negotiations between Palestine and Israel, to name a few. To keep the pressure on the president's office, many of these groups protested his perceived slowness at honoring his campaign pledges to them. The gay rights group GetEqual was particularly aggressive in this regard. While attending a fund raiser for the Democratic Party on October 11, 2010, in the backyard of former NBA star Alonzo Mourning's 12,000-square-foot mansion, GetEqual "dispatched boats into the bay adjacent to Mourning's home—equipped with bullhorns, loudspeakers, weather balloons with signs, and large banners—to get the president's attention. They said the demonstration was in protest of Mr. Obama's failure to sign an executive order barring gay and lesbian service members from being discharged under the military's 'Don't Ask, Don't Tell'" (Condon, 2010).

It was none other than openly gay member of Congress Barney Frank, who has led the charge in Congress on gay rights over the years, who tried to discourage gay rights groups from protesting in Washington in the National Equality March during Obama's first year in office. The march was designed to keep the heat on the president specifically and the Democratic Party at large to honor their campaign pledges on a host of gay issues, including doing away with the "Don't Ask, Don't Tell" law. Though Frank called the protests a "waste of time," opining that the "only thing they're [gay rights advocates] going to be putting pressure on is the grass," the march went forward (Miga, online). Judging from the Obama administration's heightened attention to gay rights issues following the march and subsequent protests (all of which have generated a considerable amount of media coverage), Frank's assessment was dead wrong. The squeaky wheel gets the grease, as the saying goes, and gay rights advocates squeaked the loudest among Obama's key constituencies and were rewarded in kind.

Maybe, then, the solution to getting Obama to develop a black agenda is to have Black America protest the Obama administration in the same ways as other groups, threatening to withhold political support if action is not taken to address their specific needs. To be fair, there has been small group protests and several members of the Congressional Black Caucus have vocally complained, but their outcry has gone mostly unheard. This outcome is not surprising, considering they have not been able to garner much support from the voting constituencies they represent. (We will revisit this tension between CBC members and Obama in chapter 5.) No doubt the bulk of Black America would shoot down the idea of mounting such a staged event. Awestruck with racial pride, most would be concerned with what type of political message such a protest would send to the GOP and the (white) American public in general. Perhaps the more pragmatic among us would argue that political solidarity is a necessary evil in this instance. Obama has little wiggle room on race matters, the thinking would go, so Black America should cut him some slack and trust that he will follow through with his campaign promises in due time. No doubt the unasked question is, What is the cost to Black America for unbridled support of the first black president? Thinking along these lines, William Jelani Cobb asks rhetorically, "What does it mean to have a black man as president when nearly a million other black men are incarcerated? When over a third of black children live below the poverty line? When nearly half the HIV deaths in the country are African American?" (164). Black America is paying too high a cost for racial pride and political solidarity when it comes to supporting Obama unconditionally. A mature black electorate must realize its voting and political power and remember what King understood all too well: "Presidents are to be held accountable, not gushed over" (143).

In many ways this issue is bigger than Obama. Looking ahead, it is very likely that Black America's treatment toward Obama will set a precedent for future dealings with black presidents. Glossed over in the media blitz following the Smiley and Sharpton debate is a profound question Smiley put to Black America: How can African Americans attempt to hold future presidents accountable for a black agenda if we do not attempt to hold Barrack Obama accountable for such an agenda? This is the question that Black America must ponder, if for no other reason than the fact that white America has already done so. (It was hardly a coincidence that the GOP elected its first black chairman of the Republican National Committee on the heels of Obama's presidential victory.) As for Smiley, squabbling over how he should or shouldn't have handled his criticism toward Obama and the black leaders that endorse Obama's post-racial philosophy on the black agenda misses the mark entirely.

At issue is how does Black America cultivate an atmosphere that allows for dissenting black voices and perspectives to be heard in a new racial environment in which a black man can become president even while major structural and racial inequalities remain largely intact. In the *Boondocks* episode McGruder addresses this issue. After Huey's unenthusiastic response of "eh," the German reporter pontificates on the bedlam that ensued: "Here is the danger of too much hope; skeptics are treated like blasphemers and indifference becomes equal to hate."

Here too is the rub when it comes to the heat Smiley has taken for his stance on Obama and the black agenda. When Obama is not factored into the equation, very few African Americans would actually disagree with Smiley's demands of the federal government. In his bestselling book *Accountable,* Smiley spells out this agenda. Specifically, he calls for a ban on racial profiling through federal law enforcement, elimination of sentencing disparities between crack and powder-based cocaine, expansion of drug courts for nonviolent offenders, job training for ex-offenders, renewable energy and infrastructure development projects for urban dwellings where the vast majority or Black America resides, lowering of health care costs, more community policing, and restoration of civil rights for disenfranchised felons who have paid their legal debt to society. Other than health care reform and a reduction (not parity) in the sentencing disparities between crack and powder cocaine, none of Smiley's crucial demands will be on the radar of the Obama administration, at least not during his first term in office and probably not during his next, assuming that he gets reelected. What Smiley understands— if inartfully articulates—is that blacks' wholesale and uncritical support of Obama contributes, directly and indirectly, to the negation of a black agenda and the maintenance of structural inequalities. By supporting Obama unconditionally, Black America is genuflecting instead of pressing for change and accountability. In the meantime, the disparities between the haves and the have-nots (of which African Americans are disproportionately represented) continue to grow. Instead of change, unconditional support of the president ensures the same subordinate social and economic status that has characterized Black America's position in the United States since its conception. And while we are under no illusion that substantive movement on these issues would occur without strong resistance and counter public policy initiatives from members of the American mainstream, inaction on advocacy for a black agenda guarantees that no progress will be made; in fact, inaction ushers in

a sense of malaise at a critical juncture for Black America. Undoubtedly, what Smiley really wants are political interest and movement on
an agenda related to structural inequalities for Black America, particularly for the poor. Ask most blacks to respond to Smiley's criticism
of President Obama and you're likely to hear a lot of people describe him
as either jealous or angry or a combination of the two. While charges
of jealousy seem farfetched at best, there is little doubt, at least from
our vantage point, that Smiley *is* angry and not *just* because Obama did
not accept his invitation to the attend his 2008 State of the Black Union
forum.[1] The more perplexing question for us, however, is not why is Tavis
Smiley so angry, but rather why is the rest of Black America so happy,[2]
especially considering the state of financial crisis that has beset a major
swath of our population, including the black middle class.

## THE END OF AMERICA

Though he has not taken as much heat[3] as Tavis Smiley, Cornel West has
been equally as critical of Obama for his inattention to the black poor
and lack of a black agenda. When asked to evaluate Obama's performance for his first year in office during an interview on *Race Talk* with
Kathleen Wells, West was visibly disappointed. Noting that he engaged
in sixty-seven pre-election presidential campaign speeches for Barack
Obama from Iowa to Ohio, West criticized Obama for neglecting policy
priorities that he pledged to deal with during the campaign. Though
West assigned Obama an "A" in terms of spiritual uplift, he assigned
him a "C-" on policy issues. West comments that enthusiasm for Obama
is starting to wane for many black people given his inaction on key issues such as employment, homes, health care and education—certainly
issues in which all Americans are concerned and need policy alternatives but that African Americans disproportionately suffer. Because
of these gross disparities, blacks also happen to be the most in need
of government intervention. Pressing West to defend his low assessment
of Obama's policy agenda for Black America and the poor, Wells asked,
"Don't you feel we're being fair to President Obama? Has any President
other than FDR been able to put working class, the poor, at the center
of their agenda?" West responds,

Well, I think LBJ actually put all the black folk, given the American apartheid
in the south and the Jim Crow junior situation in the north, at the center of his
agenda right after JFK died. And so, actually, LBJ is probably the best example,
even better than FDR, because, you remember, FDR's New Deal excluded
domestic workers and agricultural laborers, which was the vast majority of black
people. So that when you really look at the one President who has done that, it
has been LBJ in the 20th century and Lincoln in the 19th century. But Obama
talked about Lincoln, he talked about LBJ, he talked about FDR, you see? So it
was Obama who raised the hopes of the people. (Wells, online)

When Wells counters by saying that West and his supporters are
placing too high of demands on Obama because he is "only one person,"
West expounds that Obama is "not one person" but the leader of one
of the most powerful nations in the world:

He's the President who chooses an economic team that has put Wall Street and
banks at the center of their project and job creation as an afterthought—the
homes of ordinary people as an afterthought. Then he's got a foreign policy team
that chooses, and he chooses to be a war President and escalating the war, not
just in Afghanistan, but escalating those lethal drones in Pakistan. You see what
I mean?

West argues that we have to treat Obama as the powerful leader that
he is, rather than as a political operative with limited agency and authority. As for the black agenda, West opines that Obama is viewing the issue
via the eyes of his political handlers who don't fully comprehend the
legitimacy of such an agenda.

Obama has a team that understands the black agenda to be a narrow, parochial,
provincial slice of America that he can assume he always has because he's a black
President. They don't understand what black history is all about, which is that
the black agenda, from Frederick Douglass to Ida B. Wells to Martin Luther
King, has always been the most broad, deep, inclusive, embracing agenda of the
nation. Frederick Douglas's agenda was an agenda, not for black people to get out
of slavery. It was for America to become a better democracy. And it's spilt over
for women's rights; it's spilt over for worker's rights and so forth. Martin Luther
King Jr.'s agenda was not to help Negroes overcome American apartheid in the
south. It was to make America [sic] democracy a better place, where everyday
people, from poor people who were white and red and yellow and black and
brown, would be able to live lives in decency and dignity. (Wells, online)

West underscores a key point here. Namely, a black agenda is, in
fact, an American agenda and always has been. If a black agenda high-

lights the unique challenges that African Americans face, it does so, in part, because African American issues have historically been pushed to the margins of federal and state concerns. What American history teaches us on this score is simply this. White America ignores the concerns of Black America at its own social and economic peril. If, as then-senator Obama famously stated during the Democratic Presidential Convention—"There is not a Black America and a White America and Latina America and an Asian America, there is the United States of America" (Cobb, 23)—then united we stand and divided we fall. The declining state of Black America at the dawn of the twenty-first century is, in many ways, a predictor of where the rest of the country is headed if a major course change does not occur. To ignore the inextricable link between the plight of Black America and the (white) mainstream is not only unwise but dangerous.

To say that the plights of blacks and whites are inextricably linked is not to say, as Obama's post-racial policy philosophy would lead us to believe, that what's good for White America is necessarily good for Black America. Indeed, even though Obama's claim that what's good for White America is good for Black America may be true, the more crucial unasked question is "whether it was *as good* for Black America. If history was any judge, it would likely not be" (Cobb, 32). So, while issues raised by the Obama administration are useful in terms facilitating upward mobility for all of America, they do not address the particular ways in which social inequality affects black communities. This reality is precisely why America in general and Black America specifically still need a black agenda for the twenty-first century. While such an agenda would undoubtedly have positive consequences for the black poor it would target the longstanding inequalities that continue to plague the poor across racial lines.

As West rightly notes, Obama lacks even an agenda for the poor in general—a reality that is significant given that over 25 percent of African Americans fall below the poverty line according to a September 2010 Census Bureau report, and although the majority of African Americans are in the middle class, recent economic trends threaten their stability. For example, in examining unemployment rates some fifteen months after the start of the 2008 recession amongst those with a four-year college education, the Economic Policy Institute in April 2009 found that educated whites have relatively low unemployment (3.8%) in comparison to Black Americans (7.2%) with four-year college degrees (Shierholz and Edwards, online). African Americans were the target of predatory lending practices during the subprime mortgage loan crisis, including corporate banking discriminatory practices through mortgage lending at higher interest rates. This led to higher rates of foreclosure in comparison to White America. Further, Black Americans will be disproportionately affected by social security reform and attempts to roll back health care reform. Since only 2 percent of Black Americans make over $100,000 in annual income, blacks will be disproportionately impacted by tax breaks to the wealthiest Americans. In short, while White America recovers from the "Great Recession" many Black Americans have entered into the nadir of a depression not witnessed since the end of Jim Crow. The hard pill to swallow here is that Black Americans are hemorrhaging hard-gained assets and wealth during the tenure of the first black president, and this fact has barely raised an eyebrow within the mainstream American media.[4] The tragedy of this narrative is that the single person that, in theory, represents the triumphs and hopes of black political struggle in America has divested himself from this struggle as part of his political agenda. In many ways Black America has elevated Obama into the pantheon of iconoclastic black civil and human rights leadership despite the reality that, unlike these iconic black leaders who offered a moral critique of America and its (mis)treatment toward the poor, Obama has focused almost exclusively on the middle class and maintaining the status quo.

Trying to reconcile Huey's "eh" response to his question, the German reporter asks rhetorically, "So then, now that it looks like Obama is going to win as a Black African American Negro, are you merely excited or are you extremely excited that everything is going to change, forever?" When Huey responds that he thinks the declaration of a "change election" is "fake," the German reporter follows up incredulously, "So, if the election is fake then what's really going on?" Huey deadpans, "The end of America" (*Boondocks*). Even if we are not witnessing the end of America, we are certainly witnessing the end of national black politics as we know it. What should raise red flags in black spaces in regards to Obama abandoning a black agenda is the salient disconnect between whites' willingness to vote for a black president and the declining socioeconomic circumstances for African Americans in recent years. That this dynamic has barely registered as relevant in black spaces is both troubling and dangerous. If as Huey quips, "hope is irrational," it is also incredibly intoxicating, at least when it comes to Black America's unwavering support toward Obama.

# 5

## Pull Yourself Up by Your Bootstraps

*Barack Obama, the Black Poor, and the*
*Problems of Racial Common Sense Thinking*

IN 1998 TONI MORRISON declared that Bill Clinton was the nation's first black president in a *New Yorker* op-ed column, and the idea stuck in many black spaces. Though she is credited (perhaps dubiously) with introducing the idea into the mainstream, hers was merely an articulation of the admiration many African Americans felt toward Bill Clinton.[1] Though Clinton was hardly an advocate for black causes and in several critical instances actually perpetuated structural inequalities and fortified socioeconomic instability for the black poor, his salient comfort level with African Americans, individually and collectively, was truly unique. For a great majority of African Americans—who had little faith that whites would vote for a black man for president—the saxophone-playing, soul-food eating, code-switching white man with the black preacherly cadence was a welcomed phenomenon. Given Clinton's standing among blacks and the fact that a self-identified and "visibly" black candidate in Obama was vying against Clinton's wife, Hillary, for the Democratic presidential nomination and on course to make history as the "real" first black president, the comparison between Bill Clinton's symbolic blackness versus Obama's actual blackness was bound to come up. CNN news anchor Joe Johns (who also happens to be black) did the honors in a Democratic presidential debate, asking Obama "Do you think Bill Clinton was our first black president" ("Democratic Presidential Debate," online). No doubt anticipating the question and aware that many blacks were still very fond of Bill Clinton, Obama sidestepped the potentially explosive controversy with humor: "I would have to investigate more of Bill's dancing abilities, you know, and some of this other stuff before I accurately judge whether he was in fact a brother" ("Democratic Presidential Debate," online). While the questions from within black spaces over Obama's "authentic" blackness have long subsided (several prominent black figures questioned whether Obama, whose father is a black Kenyan and mother is a white American, could relate to black experiences absent a direct lineage to U.S. slavery), and those that raised them have been soundly rebuked, the pressing questions around how race generally and blackness specifically inform Obama's political calculus remain. Even as the issue of one's authentic blackness appears trivial in the so-called age of post-racialism, the ability to determine a fellow black person's politics as it pertains to dealing with White America has—and continues to be in many respects—of real social and political import. As (elite) white power[2] has been sustained in the United States from slavery to the present by a systemic practice of divide and conquer,[3] blacks have been pressed into a heightened state racial of paranoia. In *The Narrative of the Life of Frederick Douglass,* escaped slave and abolitionist Douglass (who had one of his escape attempts thwarted by a spy slave) recounts how a fellow black in the North was threatening, as a means of social leverage, to turn escaped enslaved blacks over to white authorities if they did not do his bidding. The reaction from Douglass and his black cohorts was swift and radical. They threatened him with death (some wanted to kill him outright) if he continued to put so many innocent black lives at risk for his individual and selfish pursuits. The point here is not that such a thing as "authentic blackness" exists that should necessarily distinguish one African American's perspective as more legitimate than another, but that knowing where your fellow black peer stands on issues regarding the plight of Black America—issues that up until recently were quite literally a matter of life and death[4]—remains an important factor in how blacks negotiate the politics of race in the twenty-first century.

Obama's purchase on blackness as an actual African American versus, say, Clinton's honorary blackness emerges as an important issue precisely because race continues to govern how power, status, and prestige are meted out. As America continues to navigate the most devastating economic downturn since the Great Depression, these issues of race and politics take on even greater significance. As the popular cultural saying goes, when White America catches a cold, Black America catches pneumonia. To be clear, we are making a distinction between what we call bogus notions of black authenticity and legitimate race-centric politics that aim to correct centuries of racial bias and the structural inequalities that reinforce its maintenance. Indeed, the loss of wealth and bulging wealth gap between Black and White America is more a conversation about structural economic barriers than about notions of who commands the bogus discourse on black authenticity. Skilled rhetorician and politician that he is, Obama has played fast and loose with versions of this discourse to, at once, garner black following and position himself in white spaces as an adherent of post-racial ideas of self-determination and personal responsibility (we've touched briefly on this issue in preceding chapters). Obama's political philosophy as it pertains to helping Black America has been to tether policies that help blacks to those that enjoy large white support. As we will demonstrate, this strategy is at best an updated version of an age-old (white) approach to pacifying black concerns—a phenomenon Howard Winant[5] calls the "new national [racial] 'common sense'" (115).

What we want to bring to light are how institutional norms and cultural conditions help to perpetuate inequality for many within Black America. What our analysis reveals is that even well-intentioned solutions and popular intraracial public policy alternatives that aim to remedy structural inequalities wind up doing little more than propping up the status quo. This means, to invoke the colloquium, the more things change the more they remain the same. The uncomfortable conversation the U.S. population and the Obama administration seem loathe to broach concerns how to break this cycle of poverty. Indeed, it is more politically convenient to write off the black poor as irresponsible and lazy than to own up to the fact that our capitalistic infrastructure is designed, in part, to sustain the unequal distribution of wealth. As conservative scholar Herbert Gans openly acknowledges in his research, "poverty and the poor satisfy a number of *positive* functions for many nonpoor groups in American society" (20). Stigmatized as pathological and lazy and left to basically fend for themselves in a socioeconomic structure that all but ensures they will remain in a cycle of poverty, many poor, black citizens develop conscious and unconscious oppositional coping mechanisms that range from underground illegal activities to nihilistic behaviors. The resulting "black complicity" in oppression is typically misidentified in the public discourse and has more do with structural inequalities than self-imposed victimization; an example is Daniel Patrick Moynihan's infamous description of black culture as "a tangle of pathologies" in the *The Negro Family: The Case For National Action,* 1965. In the report Moynihan blames "emasculating" black women and matriarchal family structures for black men's socioeconomic failings. The powerless are tagged not only for their plight but also for their reaction to systemic disenfranchisement (Office of Policy Planning and Research, online).

Though we take up the issue of structural inequalities for Black America, we do not intend to offer an exhaustive critique or review. There are several fine studies that cover this issue, some of which we reference throughout this chapter. Our chief goal is to discuss ways in which racialized thinking informs the maintenance of structural inequalities at the dawn of the twenty-first century, and particularly during the Obama presidency. We are especially interested in addressing extant educational disparities for Black America, including their causality and tenacity. Concomitantly, we engage a version of racial common sense thinking that informs Obama's mindset and rhetoric on such matters and that frustrates challenges to abate structural inequalities. Paradoxically speaking, racial common sense in this context means that combating racial inequality cannot come at the expense of dismantling economic power hierarchies that benefit white Americans. These incompatible goals keep structural equality always beyond reach for all but a select group of African Americans. We see racial common sense thinking at work in, say, the ways in which the Civil Rights Movement played out. Though civil rights legislation in the 1960s struck down officially sanctioned racial inequality, it did so without redistributing wealth or jeopardizing white socioeconomic control. As Derrick Bell argues in *Silent Covenants,* "relief from racial discrimination has come only when policymakers recognize that such relief will provide a clear benefit for the nation or portions of the populace. Black rights are recognized and protected when and only so long as policymakers perceive that such advances will further interests that are their primary concerns" (49).

And where does the Obama presidency fit into this schema? The maintenance of this thinking and, more specifically, structural inequalities has been carried out by every U.S. president in the modern era. Obama is no exception. In fact, he is not only the commander in chief for the country but he is also the "commander in chief of racial common sense" in the twenty-first century. Though the notion that we live in a post-racial society has been in vogue at least since the Jim Crow era, when the lines of racial discrimination were obvious for anyone with eyes to see, Obama's successful run to the White House has given the notion new life and vitality. The key difference in its popularity in the Obama era is that significant portions of blacks have bought into this thinking as well (though there is a great deal less optimism now than when Obama was first elected). Tellingly, Black America's enthusiasm for Obama's success overshadowed the harsh reality that black poverty was on the rise. In many black social and political circles, the thinking held that Obama was, at his core, a socially conscious black man who prioritized the interests of Black America, but that he couldn't always "keep it real" on race politics in the public domain because it would scare away his white supporters. The bottom line was that he was one of *us*. Not only did this racial identification mean that we need not press him to tackle black issues, but it also meant that blacks in the media and on the street who dared to criticize President Obama were "haters" or, far worse, twenty-first-century Uncle Toms. Even popular black radio personality Tom Joyner came under fire from the black community during Obama' s first year in office, when he blamed Obama's inattentiveness to black youth and the working class for why he couldn't rally blacks in key gubernatorial and Senate races in New Jersey and Massachusetts in which Democrats lost by slim margins.[6] The reality is that when it comes to the particular public policy needs of Black America, Obama thinks and responds like a politician with the black vote in his back pocket. To reiterate an earlier point, Obama believes that legislation that addresses black concerns must be smuggled in via race-neutral (read: white) initiatives in order to garner white backing and support. This position is hardly a departure from business as usual for influential, post-racial black candidates. As Manning Marble explains in *How Capitalism Underdeveloped Black America*, "In the U.S. form of constitutional government, racial minorities can influence major public policies *only* when their agenda is sufficiently acceptable to one or both of the major white capitalist parties, which in turn assimilate the proposals into their political program for their own purposes" (8, my emphasis). As we will demonstrate, Obama operates in accordance with this political calculus. It is no accident, for example, that Obama has avoided the perception of developing programs and practices crafted in favor of the particular social welfare needs of African Americans. He clearly understands that such a perception could cost him political capital and crucial white votes. On the flipside, he also understands that most black folks—another key voting bloc—will stand by him even if he largely ignores their concerns. This is not to say Obama is unaware of, or indifferent to, the problems of structural inequalities for Black America. Rather, his modus operandi is to work within the boundaries of the political system that is—and has always been—skewed largely in the favor of the white majority.[7]

In chapter 4 we discussed the dynamics of the black agenda and its role (or lack thereof) in Obama's public policy agenda. We concluded that Obama's salient resistance to embrace such an agenda played into the hands of his conservative rivals as well as buoyed the myth of a postracial America. Here, we want to focus on the socioeconomic and human costs of Obama's agenda, especially as it involves the black poor and structural inequalities. That said, we want to make clear that, however inattentive Obama has been to issues of structural inequalities in the present day, he is hardly alone in culpability. Structural inequalities were firmly entrenched in American society long before Obama assumed the mantle of power and will undoubtedly remain a thorn in the country's side long after Obama departs office (even assuming he gets reelected in 2012). To best understand how Obama fits into the bigger picture of culpability, then, one must have a grasp of how extant structural inequalities alter African American agency and self-determination even during an era when electing a black president is realizable.

In short, structural inequalities are systemic material, social, political, and economic factors that individually or in combination facilitate individual and group disadvantages. When combined with racism, structural inequalities manifest themselves in inferior housing, health services, education, and employment opportunities. As Derald Wing Sue argues in *Microaggressions in Everyday Life*, structural inequalities are often the product of institutional racism which by definition "is any policy, practice, procedure, or structure in business, industry, government, courts, churches, municipalities, schools, and so forth, by which decisions and actions are made that unfairly subordinate persons of color while allowing other groups to profit from the outcomes" (7). Consider how race figures into structural inequalities vis-à-vis mortgage loan procurement and home ownership rates in the United States. The black homeownership rate is at 47 percent compared to 49.7 percent for Hispanics and 75 percent among whites (Muhammad, online). It is harder for equally creditworthy black families to qualify for home mortgages: "black families receive far less family financial assistance with down payments and closing costs while paying higher interest rates" in comparison to white home buyers. In her article, "Presidential Address— Analysis of race and policy analysis," S. L. Myers elucidates that prior to the now famous Boston Federal Reserve Bank analyses in the 1990s on racial disparities in mortgage lending practices, the conventional wisdom was that blacks and Hispanics received low rates of mortgage credit because they had lower credit scores. However, the Boston Federal Reserve Bank analysis found that although blacks and Hispanics had lower credit scores when compared to whites, when controlling for credit risk due to low credit scores, blacks and Hispanics were still less likely to obtain mortgage loans. The analysis, then, determined that racial discrimination accounted for racial gaps in mortgage lending practices.

There are, of course, multiple other indicators of structural inequalities, some of which we have alluded to in previous chapters. For instance, for every dollar of net worth (the sum of a family's assets less its debt) that Anglo Americans have, Hispanic Americans have 9 cents and African Americans have approximately 7 cents. While African Americans tend to start more entrepreneurial business opportunities than their Anglo American cohorts, entrepreneurship brings less wealth to blacks when compared to whites. The wealth advantage for white entrepreneurs over white workers is $226,382 versus $108,285, while the wealth advantage for black entrepreneurs over black workers is $64,506 versus $27,244 (Bradford, online).

Residential segregation is another "hidden-in-plain-sight" variable that disadvantages African American populations. Indeed, three quarters of Black America live in segregated communities. Discussing residential segregation in his insightful book *The Hidden Cost of Being African American*, Thomas Shapiro points out that "no other group experiences segregation to the extent that blacks do" (141). This reality flies in the face of mainstream knowledge about African American integration. In truth, residential segregation remains a powerful force that presents multiple challenges that often undermine the well being of blacks. As Shapiro further explains, "The residential color line means that blacks have greater difficulty overcoming problems associated with poor communities, especially crime, violence, housing abandonment, unstable families, poorer health and higher mortality, environmental degradation, and failing schools" (141).

To get a fuller understanding of the tenacity of structural inequalities, one needs to understand the deleterious impact of slavery on African American achievement, wealth, and prosperity. One also needs to understand how whites in the present day continue to benefit from slavery—socially, economically, and culturally—even absent the overt racial markers of discrimination that were in place throughout the better part of the twentieth century. To refer again to Shapiro, "Many whites continue to reap advantages from the historical, institutional, structural, and personal dynamics of racial inequality, and they are either unaware of these advantages or deny they exist" (13). This aspect of white privilege not only explains the Obama Administration's silences on this issue, but it also explains the silence in the media and the public discourse at large. For example, when on the rare occasions the issue of structural inequalities comes up for public debate, it tends to focus on the plight of white Americans, not people of color. Consider for instance Glenn Beck's "Restoring Honor Movement" in which he egregiously rewrites civil rights history, positioning Tea Partiers (the overwhelming majority of whom are ultraconservative, upper-middle-class whites) as civil rights pioneers and the burden bearers of structural inequalities in the country. Or consider the ways in which the popular media covered (over) black experiences during the "Great Recession." If they relied solely on these media for their news—which sadly most U.S. citizens do—most would be surprised to learn that the black unemployment rate in several major metropolitan areas was nearly twice as high as the national average and that the subprime mortgage scandal was far more economically devastating for people of color than for whites.

These racial blind spots on structural inequalities are not just evident in the media. They are written into the DNA of our cultural identity. A prime example is the way the historical notion of blacks' "progress" in the United States is divorced from extant structural inequalities. Because the study of black history in the public discourse is inextricably and parochially tied to blacks acquiring freedom and civil rights, the economic variables that are equally, if not more important, to black self-determination—then and now—fall through the cracks of serious consideration. As Manning Marable observes,

> The study of Black social stratification and political economy departs from an appreciation of the contours of Black history. Yet where we stand in the past largely determines our understanding of what a people have been, and what they intend to become. Beneath history exists explicitly or implicitly a philosophy or worldview that tends to explain or to justify phenomena. All history conceals an a priori superstructure which promotes the interests of certain social classes at the expense of others. (18)

Indeed, there is a growing wealth gap within Black America. At one extreme, 'African American income levels are rising faster than average with close to two million African American households registering incomes of at least $75,000. The aggregate income of most affluent Black families is at $116 billion and climbing. The number of African American homeowners has grown by a third in the last decade (Shapiro). At the other extreme are the facts provided in a September 2010 U.S. Census Bureau Report, which cites that in 2009, 25.8 percent of blacks were below the poverty line as compared to 25.3 percent of Hispanics, and 9.4 percent of white non-Hispanics. This is a change in one year of 1.1 percent for Black America from 24.7 percent in 2008. What's more, the majority of low-income black Americans live within inner-city and urban dwellings where approximately 70 percent of African Americans reside. The bulk of this urban poverty is directly tied to the lost of urban manufacturing jobs. "In the twenty-year period from 1967 to 1987, Philadelphia lost 94 percent of its manufacturing jobs; Chicago lost 60 percent; New York City, 58 percent; [and] Detroit, 51 percent (Stoesz, 137). As it presently stands, 50 percent of black youth living in major metropolitan areas cannot find employment. According to an October 2009 report from the Bureau of Labor Statistics, 17.3 percent of black males over the age of 20 were unemployed as compared to 10.7 percent of white men over 20. Similarly, black women over the age of 20 had a 13.3 percent unemployment rate while the rate for white women over the age of 20 is 7.1 percent. The black unemployment rate for those 16–19 was 43.5 percent while the rate for whites between the same age ranges is 24.1 percent.

The manifestation of these structural inequalities continues on Obama's watch. Though the popular perspective among African Americans is that Obama prioritizes black concerns, the reality is far less romantic. Indeed, in *The Audacity of Hope,* Obama operates from a logic of racial common sense that unburdens whites from direct responsibility for structural inequalities, blaming instead what he refers to as "entrenched behavioral patterns among the black poor" (254). More specifically, Obama argues in support of Daniel Patrick Moynihan's controversial 1960s report on the status of Black America. Bucking with civil rights leaders and what he calls "liberal policymakers," Obama decries the accusation that Moynihan's report was inaccurate and racist. In a rather stunning analysis, Obama concurs with Moynihan that self-destructive behavior on the part of the black poor (the aforementioned "tangle of pathologies") was the chief contributor to black socioeconomic struggles in the first half of the twentieth century. Tellingly, though, Obama does not rehearse Moynihan's explosive lexicon when it comes to describing blacks' behavior. That is, he doesn't describe blacks as inherently pathological. But, of course, Obama's doesn't have to say it. Moynihan has already done the dirty work, so to speak. By siding with Moynihan and the dressed-up Horatio Alger myth that undergirds his assessment of black pathology, Obama scores political points with moderate white Democrats and Republicans that see self-help models as the panacea for black socioeconomic struggles. Judging from the fact that he's experienced little, if any, blowback from this controversial endorsement (we may, in fact, be the first to raise the issue at all), it clearly

separated him from the herd of identifiable black and victim-centric candidates in a way that maximized political effect at a minimal political
cost. In political-speak, it was a homerun.

Political strategy aside, Obama's endorsement of the Moynihan report provides critical insight into his thinking about the African American poor and the root cause of structural inequalities. While Obama
is clearly comfortable with highlighting aspects of black complicity in
oppression, he is decidedly uncomfortable with holding white America
accountable. Consider the following passage from his "Race" chapter in
*Audacity of Hope:*

> An emphasis on universal, as opposed to race-specific, programs isn't just good
> policy; it's also good politics. I remember once sitting with one of my democratic
> colleagues in the Illinois state senate as we listened to another fellow senator—
> an African American whom I'll call John Doe who represented a largely inner-
> city district—launch into a lengthy and passionate peroration on why the elimi-
> nation of a certain program was a case of blatant racism. After a few minutes, the
> white senator (who had one of the chamber's more liberal voting records) turned
> to me and said, "You know what the problem is with John? Whenever I hear him,
> he makes me feel more white." (247)

Here, the problems of Obama's racial common sense are thrown
radically into focus. He clearly sides with a liberal white senator's assessment regarding a black senator's spirited charge of racism regarding
the elimination of an unnamed social program in his district. The white
senator finds the black senator's peroration distasteful, remarking that
it makes him "feel more white." The twisted moral to Obama's anecdote
is that the best way to form coalitions with whites is to avoid invoking race in ways that may offend them. His rationale is that white guilt
"has largely exhausted itself in America," meaning that even justified
appeals for racial equality are met with resistance or hostility. The trick
for Obama is to find common ground on race issues as a strategy to gain
white political support on legislation that is "race neutral" but disproportionately aids Black America.

Upon first glance, this approach seems politically practical, if not
shrewd, given the disparity in power and critical mass. African Americans are simply not in the social or political position to force legislation
through or to dictate the terms of the public discourse. Closer scrutiny,

however, reveals the problems with his thinking. However well intentioned and strategic, Obama's racial common sense compromise does far
more harm than good when it comes to black empowerment. While it is
true that blacks have limited power and agency, they can ill afford to give
whites the power to control or rewrite the narrative of the black agenda.
Would the liberal white senator have felt less "white" or threatened by the
black senator's statements if he had first acknowledged that not all white
people are racist or if he had emphasized—like Obama is prone to doing—that blacks must shoulder some, if not most, of the blame for per-
petuating structural inequalities? Moreover, is anger not an appropriate
response to blatant racial oppression? Certainly, history demonstrates
that reform happens, not when the oppressed operates according to the
dictates of the oppressors but when they organize, strategize, and fight
back. To depend on (liberal) whites' goodwill to carry the day for Black
America seems not only naïve but dangerous.

There are other ways in which Obama's racial common sense falls
flat as it pertains to blacks and ending structural inequalities. His education reform is perhaps the most problematic in this regard. At the
top of his political agenda as a presidential candidate, Obama pledged
that education reform would be a top priority. True to his racial common sense mode of thinking, Obama pitched his educational initiative,
Race to the Top, as a race-neutral program that would improve public
education for all Americans. While there is no debating that national
education reform is sorely needed across the board, urban black Americans are disproportionately disadvantaged by educational inequalities.
This statistical reality is rendered invisible via Obama's racial common sense thinking. Indeed, what many Obama supporters may not
know is that his highly touted education reforms are largely in sync
with George W. Bush's much maligned No Child Left Behind policy
(hereafter NCLB). NCLB emerged during the Bush administration as the
signature public policy plan to reduce disparities in education outcomes.
"Conservatives backed NCLB because of its mandate for accountability
through standardized testing, teacher certification, and reform of failing schools. Liberals endorsed it because it pinpointed issues of equality
such as smaller school classrooms, professional development for teachers, teacher certification, after-school care, and youth safety programs"

(Teasley, 25). Former Bush-era assistant secretary of education Diane Ravitch dropped a bombshell, pointing out that the achievement gaps between black and white students narrowed more *before* the implementation of NCLB than in the years afterward. Black fourth-grade students produced a 13-point gain in math testing scores from 2000 to 2003 but only a 6-point gain from 2003 to 2006. In many areas across grade levels, there was no gain in student achievement scores.

For many conservatives, school choice is the idealized method for market-based reform through the promotion of self-help. The conservative rationale behind school vouchers and charter schools is that students residing in low-income areas receiving education in failing schools will have the opportunity to succeed in new schools based on marketplace choice and parental commitment to educational excellence. Disguised as a method of providing school choice for poor children in failing school systems, the Bush administration attempted to usher in a school voucher system with the ultimate goal of reducing federal spending on public education. But the voucher debate ran into several political and judicial roadblocks. Chief among them was that the public did not endorse market reform through the use of school vouchers. The most outspoken opponents of this market reform were concerned that school vouchers would bankrupt funding for public schools.

Obama picked up where Bush left off, continuing and enhancing NCLB through his Race to the Top program. For example, Race to the Top calls for greater school-choice measures, including evaluating teachers in relation to student's standardized testing scores, handing public schools that continue to get low test scores to private management (possibly as charter schools), and firing school administrators and teachers in low-performing schools. In *The Death and Life of the Great American School System: How Testing and Choice Are Undermining Education,* Ravitch reports that when federal support for vouchers shifted to the implementation of a charter school system as the vehicle to inject competition and market forces into American education, the Obama administration accommodated this policy shift by urging state legislatures to remove their caps on charter schools. The Department of Education under the Obama administration favored the expansion of charter schools and advised states that they must eliminate legal limits on the expansion of charter schools to be eligible for nearly $5 billion in discretionary funds. Ravitch, a renowned scholar in education policy, sees this move as puzzling, considering Obama's campaign pledges on education: "Here was a president who had been elected on a promise of change, yet he was picking up the same banner of choice competition, and markets that had been the hallmark of his predecessors" (146). In a related essay, "In Need of a Renaissance: Real Reform Will Renew, Not Abandon, Our Neighborhood Schools," Ravitch warns of looming disaster in the move to market-based education reform based on the expansion of charter schools:

> The question for the future is whether the continued growth of charter schools in urban districts will leave regular public schools with the most difficult students to educate, thus creating a two-tier system of widening inequality. If so, we can safely predict that future studies will "prove" the success of charter schools and the failure of regular schools, because the public schools will have disproportionate numbers of less motivated parents and needier students. (14)

The "needier students" Ravitch speaks of are disproportionately the black poor in urban communities who have fewer resources and will least likely benefit from the development of a privatized charter school system. In or out of a charter school system, the goal will be to minimize tax-funded dollars on per pupil spending. Already, children who need the most in school resources start out at the worse schools. "Schools in better-off districts spend more money per student than schools in lower-income areas. In actual dollars spent per pupil for educational expenses, the richest school districts spend 56 percent more per student than the nation's poorest districts" (Shapiro, 145). Thus, the move to a majority charter school system threatens to exacerbate an already bleak outlook. It is quite revealing that powerful private foundations with vested interest, along with right-wing political think tanks, support the Obama administration's education policies and are behind efforts to privatize schools in cities like Detroit, St Louis, New Orleans, New York City, and Washington, DC (Noguera).

Basically, what we find is that although public schools have become much more segregated since the Supreme Court changed the law in the 1990s, charter schools are even vastly more segregated. And this segregation is not just by race but also by poverty. There are segregated black schools, some segregated Latino schools, and segregated white schools that *over-represent* middle-class whites in some states (including California), some of which appear to have no free lunch facility. So, basically, the system of choice that is used here does not have the civil rights protections that good magnet schools have. And the Bush administration, as it pushed the growth of these policies, really stopped trying to enforce civil rights in this movement. Obama's one-size-fits-all model leaves the most vulnerable black urban populations at risk for further poor education outcomes.[8] Suffice it to say, that Race to the Top will not fix the long-standing problems of educating urban Black America. What is clearly needed to rectify this race and class divide in educational outcomes is a policy uniquely tailored to the circumstances and obstacles for the urban black poor. Obama's racial common sense thinking is harmful, then, on one level because it impedes consideration of the very things (in this case race and class) that are necessary to diagnose and potentially solve structural educational inequalities.

Another reason that Obama's racial common sense thinking must be seriously scrutinized is that it reinforces skewed black neoconservative arguments that blacks are fully culpable for academic underachievement and self-determination. Within this framework of thinking, to hold whites responsible for black educational underachievement is to ignore or squander the gains of the Civil Rights Movement. While addressing black complicity in oppression is a useful and necessary endeavor, this conservative discourse of self-help leads away from, rather than toward, productive solutions to reduce inequalities. Ron Christie's book, *Acting White: The Curious History of a Racial Slur*, is instructive in this regard. A black political analyst and former White House consultant for the Bush administration, Christie uncovers what he refers to as the historical origins of the connotation of "acting white"—the notion that trying hard in school means a betrayal of black culture and authenticity. Relying chiefly on anecdotal evidence, including his feelings of cultural alienation as a black Republican, Christie arrives at the convenient conclusion that "acting white"—not structural inequalities—is the primary reason for black/white educational disparities. Echoing the black neoconservative sentiments of John McWhorter, Shelby Steele, and, more recently, Bill Cosby, Christie sees the *Brown vs. Board of Education* decision as having leveled the educational playing field for Black America. What this means, at bottom, is that underachieving blacks (most of whom are poor) have only themselves to blame for why they are being "left behind":

> More than fifty years following the historic Brown v. Board of Education decision that outlawed separate but equal accommodations as offensive to the equal protection of law under the Constitution, a new form of segregation now sweeps across America. In a disturbing trend, many blacks mock members of their own race who seek academic excellence in the classroom and speak and dress well as being nothing more than Uncle Toms and acting white. (154)

From Christie's reductive and ahistorical vantage point, blacks have developed a pathological mindset (think Moynihan report) divorced from the material realities of institutional white oppression, wherein they police underachievement by impugning black high achievers as racial sellouts. The driving force behind this policing of underachievement is a discourse of what he calls "black authenticity." Christie sees black authenticity as the opposite of acting white. That is, black authenticity is tethered to the pathological notion that high educational achievement bespeaks a desire to assimilate whiteness. In effect, authentic blacks are unassimilated blacks who reject all forms of white accommodationism, including high achievement in schools. Christie couches black authenticity as a manifestation of self-imposed victimhood, resulting from regressive "Negro thinking." In his formulation, hustling and criminal activities become the authenticating behavior of blacks.

That there is such a thing as an "acting white" discourse cannot be denied. The problem, however, is that Christie collapses the cause and effect of the discourse, making it appear that "acting white" stems from inherently pathological thinking rather than from a reaction to conspicuous white privilege and institutionalized white oppression. In truth, "acting white"—which is far more complex that Christie describes (for there are always competing discourses of black achievement even in spaces where the acting white phenomenon is at play)—is perhaps best explained as a coping mechanism and not as a diagnosis for academic underachievement. If, indeed, one perceives that the doors of opportunity are shut off, it makes perfect sense to develop an oppositional identity to shield oneself from feelings of intellectual inadequacy and racial inferiority.

Christie's uncritical, if not outlandish, analysis stokes the fire of his conservative bent and disregards the lingering effects of structural in-equalities on Black America. The irony is that Christie's "blackness" is what fundamentally "authenticates" his twisted view of black realities (at least in the eyes of post-racialists across political, class, and race lines). Hardly an expert in African American studies, Christie no more speaks for Black America than do the "authentic blackness" proponents that he summarily blames and attacks. Christie's reliance on individual experi-ence to make pseudo-empirical claims about black educational under-achievement is not only shortsighted but counterproductive. He paints a picture of black authenticity in the form of what Robin D. G. Kelley refers to tongue-and-cheek as "the real Negroes," those who are "young [and] jobless with the nastiest verbal repertoire, the pimps and hustlers, and the single mothers who raised streetwise kids who began cursing before they could walk" (20). In doing so, Christie encourages the type of scapegoating and reductive view of black humanity that allows many whites to ignore their participation in the maintenance of structural inequalities. Portraits of the urban black poor as ambivalent about edu-cational attainment based on the radicalized notion of acting white are shallow, convenient, and part of a post-racial mindset that conflates ra-cial common sense thinking with the political legitimacy to promote individuality and self-reliance as the prescription to unabated, intergen-erational poverty for Black America.

The fact that Christie invokes Obama to defend his claims about black pathology and "acting white" is telling on a number of political fronts. Christie's conservative political motivations are clear. He wants to paint Obama and his supporters as hypocritical on the issues of edu-cational achievement and black self-determination by demonstrating that he and Obama are actually on the same page when it comes to as-sessing why black children do not succeed on the level of their white peers in school. More specifically, Christie offers "proof" of his claims by referencing Obama's iconic 2004 speech at the Democratic National Convention (which catapulted him to national prominence) in which Obama attacks the "acting white" thinking in black spaces:

> Go into any inner-city neighborhood, and folks will tell you that government alone can't teach kids to learn. They know that parents have to teach, that

children can't achieve unless we raise their expectations and turn off the television sets and eradicate the slander that says a black youth with a book is acting white. They know those things. (Obama quoted in Christie, 162)

While Christie's political motivations are certainly questionable, his criticism of Obama has legitimacy. Of course, the pertinent point here is not that Obama and his supporters are hypocrites but that Obama's views about (poor) black educational underachievement, self-determination, and acting white are strikingly similar to those of neoconservatives like Christie.

The "unasked question" that emerges, to borrow Du Bois's words in *The Souls of Black Folk,* is why, given Obama's conservatism on issues of black achievement and structural inequalities, do blacks not question his sincerity or political agenda. This is a crucial question for a number of reasons, the most important being that if blacks remain on their current socioeconomic decline under the Obama administration (a decline which predates Obama's presidency) they will be *far worse off* when Obama leaves office than when his presidency began. This is the ugly truth that Black America seems reluctant to fully appreciate or engage. Suffice it to say that this is a complex matter with lots of moving parts. It is not enough to say that blacks are enthralled with Barack Obama only because he is black. As we discussed earlier, the shallowness of such a claim becomes clear when considering that whites—not blacks—are the ones that have historically exhibited racial biases in the voting booth (consider the notorious "Bradley Effect" that was bandied about in the media during Obama's presidential campaign).[9] Moreover, the strategic selection of the first African American chairman of the Republican National Committee in Michael Steele did nothing to alter the overwhelming perception of the GOP as insensitive to the concerns of Black America. The truth of the matter is that Obama is "identifiably black" on a number of political and cultural fronts that resonate with many African Americans. From his famous fist bumps with Michelle, love of hip hop and gospel music, and admiration of black women with curves, to his fluid vernacular code switching, Obama performs an uptown/downtown blackness that gives him political and cultural purchase across socioeconomic status. He strikes a chord with blacks, say, in the same classed and peculiar ways that Ronald Reagan and George

W. Bush struck a chord with whites across class lines. And, in many ways, the stakes for blacks in throwing their unconditional support behind Obama is as high as those working-class whites during the Reagan and Bush years who often voted against their best socioeconomic interests.

Ironically enough, it is another white man in Bill Clinton that provides the cautionary tale for why Black America should become more critical in their thinking about Obama. Prior to Obama's rise, Clinton occupied the most esteemed position in Black America for a president. As noted earlier, Nobel Prize–winning author Toni Morrison went so far as to identify Clinton as the "first black president"—an idea that allowed Clinton to maintain favor with Black America and substantiate his commitment to fighting structural inequalities even as he pushed through policies that actually intensified those inequalities. Indeed, while the "comeback kid" gave the appearance of being "pro-black" through government appointments and other actual and symbolic gestures, he continued the pattern of racial common sense thinking of his predecessors. What constituted Clinton's blackness, according to Morrison (who now claims that her statements were taken out of context), was his single-parent upbringing, working-class status, saxophone playing skills, junk-food eating habits, and, most importantly, his vulnerability to white conservative attack. If anything, Clinton played up these characteristics after Morrison's curious declaration and, on frequent occasions, used it as political capital to get blacks behind even some of his most damaging public policies, including the outcomes of his welfare reform agenda for Black America. If we put Clinton's track record with Black America under the microscope, we don't see a radical departure from the ways in which white presidents—be they Democratic or Republican—have dealt with the public policy needs of Black America since the Lyndon B. Johnson administration in the 1960s.

The impact of Clinton's public policies on Black America has been painful and lasting. For example, the Clinton administration enacted the largest crime bill in history with the 1994 Violent Crime Control Law Enforcement Act. It provided $9.7 billion in funding for prisons and enacted the "three strikes you're out" law that led to massive incarceration of nonviolent offenders. It also put an end to Pell Grant eligibility for prisoners and cut prison education programs. To date, more than 80 percent of those sentenced under the law are African American and Hispanic. Even Janet Reno, Clinton's attorney general at the time, recognized the problems of the policy, stating that the sentencing disparity between powder cocaine and crack cocaine was unfair. But the certified "black president" was to inaugurate one of the harshest social policy measures for Black America in the latter part of the twentieth century. On August 22, 1996, he signed into law the Personal Responsibility and Work Opportunity Reconciliation Act (PRWORA) in order to, in his words, end "welfare as we know it" and replaced it with a block grant to states called Temporary Assistance to Needy Families (TANF).

Clinton's framed the policy in moral terms, seeking to, as some pundits quipped, to "out conserve" the conservatives—a move that was politically expedient given his multiple sex scandals and need to remake his public image. While Clinton argued that his welfare reform policies would have mutual benefits for employees and employers alike, the reality was less encouraging. Many companies that endorsed TANF legislation foresaw financial gain from greater access to TANF recipients as cheap labor. In contrast, TANF recipients gained little in terms of career employment opportunities and most stayed below the poverty line. As stated in a 2004 U.S. Department of Labor report, "employers interested in hiring TANF recipients are more likely to be offering jobs with irregular work hours, low pay, and/or alternative job arrangements" (Long and Ouellette, 18). As a national effort to prompt the poor to engage in self-help through employment, TANF replaced the longstanding Aid to Families with Dependent Children program. It forced program participants to work in order to receive benefits and services, denied benefits to legal immigrants, and cut funding for low-income programs to include food stamps and the Supplemental Security Income, which provided benefits for the disabled poor and the elderly. In *Quixote's Ghost: The Right, the Liberati, and the Future of Social Policy*, social policy expert David Stoesz explains that "the typical welfare-to-work program increases participants' income, but only by several hundred dollars annually, hardly enough to make families self-sufficient. Moreover, savings to welfare departments are modest [and] the earnings do little to lift welfare recipients out of poverty" (174).

Three years after the passing of the PRWORA, only 23 percent of those moving off of AFDC to work were still employed. The state of Florida, for example, witnessed a decrease in the monthly family income from $913.20 to $756.20. In order to generate income, approximately two-fifths (39 percent) of welfare recipients "worked off the books or under a false identity to generate additional income and 8 percent worked in the underground economy selling sex, drugs, or stolen goods" (Stoesz, 138). In order to make ends meet, 77 percent of mothers received covert contribution from absent fathers, boyfriends, or family. Thus, while the national public assistance rolls declined "over time with the percent of the poor dropping from 56 percent in the first year [of PRWORA] to 41 percent in the fifth year [of the program] more than half (54.6 percent) of mothers were independent of public assistance altogether, although only one third, 35.8 percent, were above the poverty line on the basis of their income alone" (140).

During the reauthorization of PRWORA in 2001 in Congress, the White House and supporters of the social policy claimed success on the basis that overall public assistance rolls had declined. Tellingly, there was no report on the aforementioned distributing trend of "covert work" to maintain families. The results of the national self-help program via the 1996 PRWORA were disastrous for Black America in multiple ways. As Stoesz rightly notes, "Neither welfare nor work was sufficient to provide for their families, so mothers overlapped and augmented them" (140). In other words, in order to survive these mothers and welfare recipients were pressed into participation in underground markets and illegal economies. The untold story of Clinton's welfare reform policies was that it became a catalyst for criminal activity within low-income black communities. Moreover, the influx of black men into the criminal justice system left scores of black children fatherless and escalated the number of impoverished, single women–led homes. Though Clinton claimed to encourage marriage and stable family structures with the enactment of TANF, the policy exacerbated an already troubling trend in Black America. The 2009 census data revealed that 60 percent of homes led by black single female parents are below the poverty line.

In "The Clinton Fallacy: Did Blacks Really Make Big Economic Gains during the '90s?" renowned scholar Melissa Harris-Perry offers a useful summary of how Clinton managed to maintain black loyalty despite introducing such socially and economically debilitating policies:

> The hypnotic racial dance of cultural authenticity that Bill Clinton performed in office lulled many blacks into a perceptual fog. Clinton actively cultivated a unique and intense relationship with black voters. He relished this bond and often acknowledged his honorary blackness. As Clinton performed blackness, real black people got poorer. The poorest African-Americans experienced an absolute decline in income, and they also became poorer relative to the poorest whites. The richest African-Americans saw an increase in income, but even the highest-earning blacks still considerably lagged their white counterparts. Furthermore, the '90s witnessed the continued growth of the significant gap between black and white median wealth. (online)

Harris-Perry further notes that when she studied trends in blacks' support of Clinton she found that as much as 30 percent of his supporters "held false understandings of black economic conditions during the Clinton years" (online). She reports that by the time Clinton left office this significant segment of African Americans wrongly believed that blacks were doing better economically than whites. This is a striking case of misinformation, considering that in the 1980s "barely 5 percent of blacks believed blacks were economically better off than whites" (online). The reality, of course, is that "there is no evidence to suggest that African-Americans were in better economic position than whites at any time in American history, including during the Clinton presidency" (online). Beyond keeping inflation low and reducing unemployment, Clinton did not radically alter the socioeconomic reality of Black America. In terms of structural inequalities, he clearly did more harm than good. That blacks were so enthralled with him as president, then, is clearly more attributable to his charisma and conspicuous comfort level in black spaces than to his actual social policies. What this demonstrates in rather dramatic fashion are the measurable ways in which Clinton harnessed black goodwill for political gain.

## OBAMA AND SYMBOLIC BLACKNESS

What Bill Clinton quickly discovered in 2008 as he campaigned vigorously in support of his wife, Hillary Clinton, for the Democratic presidential nomination was that symbolic blackness was no substitute for the real thing. Seeking to downplay the shellacking that Hillary received in South Carolina from Obama—especially among black voters—Clinton compared Obama's victory to that of Jesse Jackson's in 1984 and 1988. Though in the public domain Clinton repeatedly denied his obvious racial swipe, suggesting that Obama's victory in South Carolina, like Jackson's in '84 and '88, was largely meaningless beyond a show of racial solidarity, black folks were none too happy with his racial shenanigans and reflected their feelings at the voting booth and over the airwaves. The limits of Clinton's symbolic blackness had become exposed.

Obama, of course, did not start out as a fan favorite among African Americans. Prior to his surprising win in the Democratic primary in Iowa, few African Americans even knew who he was. The buzz within black spaces was not over the possibility of electing the nation's first black president, but over whether Obama—who has an African father and white American mother—was even "authentically" black. These debates over his black authenticity all but vanished once he won the Iowa caucus in one of the whitest states in the country. Instantly grasping the significance of the political moment, African Americans flocked to Obama's camp in droves. To the dismay of many of the civil rights stalwarts who were either throwing their support behind Hillary Clinton, like Andrew Young, or waiting on the sidelines hedging their bets, like Jesse Jackson, Obama was locking up the black vote without their intervention or endorsement: "Positioned as he was between the black boomers and the hip hop generation, Obama was indebted, but not beholden, to the civil rights gerontocracy. A successful Obama candidacy would simultaneously represent a huge leap forward for black America and the death knell for the civil-rights-era leadership" (Cobb, 65–66). Indeed, the civil rights gerontocracy of which Jackson and Young were major players operated from their own version of racial common sense. For their generation, a sign of political maturity was the "ability to extract concessions" from whites. The problem with this logic—as Obama revealed in his successful run to the presidency—was that it "operated on the tacit assumption that the most any black leader could aspire to was influence over more powerful white ones" (65). Obama's success demonstrated that this brand of racial common sense was outdated. While on its face, this shift seemed rather significant, it hardly represented a radical departure from the racial common sense of old. As Obama's aforementioned rationale on courting white liberal votes clearly attests, he still believes that the path to political success goes through elite and powerful whites. The irony is that in this regard his racial common sense thinking is very much in line with the civil rights gerontocracy. He just recognized— earlier than most—that a black man could be atop the ticket despite the extant racial and economic reality of white power.

Unfortunately for Black America, Obama has used his political capital as a black man in much the same questionable ways that Clinton used his symbolic blackness. The Congressional Black Caucus learned this lesson the hard way when it pressed for Obama to address the disproportionate ways that blacks have been impacted by the Great Recession and subprime mortgage fallout in his 2010 State of the Union speech. Clearly unfazed by the pressure from the CBC to distinguish the unique challenges facing Black America and the poor during the recession, Obama avoided even mentioning the words "black," "African American," or "poverty" in his speech. More specifically, he punted on addressing the unflattering socioeconomic realities that continue to sustain structural inequalities and that disproportionately affect many minority communities. He also did not prepare the nation for the somber realities of the Great Recession in terms of its full impact on the economy, including the dismal economic projections, the dilemmas facing the monetary supply, and the tepid outlook for job growth.

Though it has generated virtually no media attention, Obama's relationship with the Congressional Black Caucus has been largely contemptuous from the outset of his presidency. After receiving nearly 95 percent of the black vote, many members of the caucus all but demanded that Obama honor the overwhelming support he received from African Americans by making their concerns a priority in his economic agenda. This demand was certainly warranted considering the crumbling state of Black America as Obama entered office. After the 2008 financial crash, large numbers of Black Americans found themselves on the short end of the economic downturn. At the start of the recession in December

2007, black unemployment was recorded at 8 percent but escalated to 15.8 percent by December 2009 with 34.5 percent of black Americans ages 16–24 unemployed. In comparison, the rate for whites in December 2009 was 9.3 percent, for Hispanics 12.7 percent, and Asians 7.3 percent (Goldman, online). Even Washington, DC, which fared well during the start of the Great Recession, found itself with a jobless rate of 34.5 percent for black males ages 16–24 in October 2009. To date, many of the largest urban areas throughout the country have black male unemployment rates of 40 and 50 percent.

Dissatisfaction with Obama's inattention to the overwhelming problems of the national black unemployment rate boiled over in December 2009 when 10 members of the CBC protested a House Committee vote on financial reform. Black lawmakers complained of being ignored and slighted through cancellation of appointments and slow returns on phone calls. One of the chief grievances included an initial[10] snub to senior CBC members from the White House regarding their request for a meeting to discuss Obama's public policy agenda for job creation in Black America. Obama opted instead to have a closed-door meeting with civil rights leaders and newly acquired political allies Al Sharpton, Benjamin Jealous, and Marc Morial. Another rift between CBC and Obama involved his stealth political maneuver to get David Patterson, then-Democratic governor of New York, to drop his reelection bid. Even seemingly small requests from the CBC were ignored, like the request for Rep. Donna Christensen, a physician, to be included in the 2009 White House health care summit. Commenting on the White House's indifference to CBC's concerns in a March 2010 *Politico* article, Lisa Lerer and Nia-Malika Henderson observe that "unlike previous presidents, Obama doesn't need to win over the CBC in order to pick up support in the black community. Polls show that 96 percent of black voters view him favorably—a number that CBC representatives probably can't match themselves" (online). Providing further commentary on this state of affairs, public policy scholar Michael Fauntroy asserts, "The sense I get is that [black] people are far more protective of President Obama than they are of their own representatives that they have known for 20 years" (online). Lerer and Henderson report that this point was not lost on Obama in their interview. Obama boasted about his polling numbers among blacks when discussing the grumblings among the black leadership in the CBC. Obama displays this sentiment rather boldly in an interview with April Ryan of American Urban Radio Networks: "If you want me to line up all the black actors, for example, who support me, and put them on one side of the room, and a couple who are grumbling on the other, I'm happy to have that. I think if you look at the polling, in terms of the attitudes of the African-American community, there's overwhelming support for what we've tried to do" (Ryan, online).

Despite the fact that the poll numbers are indeed in Obama's favor, the grievances from the CBC should not be overlooked. Even Rep. Jesse Jackson Jr.—a staunch Obama ally, who even took his famous father to task for derogatory comments he made about Obama during the presidential campaign—has been critical of Obama's handling of black unemployment and working-class issues: "While I respect President Obama, delivering victories for his political future should be the least of our worries on Capitol Hill" ("Jesse Jr: Obama's 'political future' not my top concern."). House Judiciary Committee Chairman John Conyers and Rep. Alcee Hasting have been outspoken as well, arguing that Obama is not listening to black lawmakers' concerns about the black poor. Democratic Rep. Maxine Waters of California has made the most ruckus and endured the most political heat. Holding firm to her political commitment to black communities, she has challenged the president directly, proclaiming, "We're out of the box, we're full speed ahead and we are not going to sit back and watch our communities suffer in silence" (Edney, online). Waters's remarks were part of an effort by CBC members to boycott a 2009 House Financial Services Committee vote in order to gain attention for their concerns. Representative Walters further remarked, "We have cooperated with the leadership. We have cooperated with the administration. We have supported the bailout and now we're saying, 'What do we get for all of this cooperation? What are we delivering to our communities?' And the answer is little or nothing" (Edney, online).

The CBC pushed for efforts to reduce home foreclosures, to improve credit access for black-owned auto dealerships, to expand aid to small and medium community banks, and to obtain federal money to support the purchase of black newspapers and radio stations. In response to the demands of the CBC, Obama actually agreed that aiding black businesses is important but only as a part of a larger race neutral and inclusive strategy to get all American businesses up and running again. Offering a now familiar retort to such racial concerns, he opined,

> I will tell you that I think the most important thing I can do for the African-American community is the same thing I can do for the American community, period, and that is get the economy going again and get people hiring again. And, I think it's a mistake to start thinking in terms of particular ethnic segments of the United States rather than to think that we are all in this together and we are all going to get out of this together. (Jackson, online)

Obama's racial common sense and one-size-fits-all philosophy simply doesn't bode well for Black America in real economic terms. Using data gathered from the federal Small Business Association, the New America Media reported in December 2009 that minority businesses were nearly shut out of 2008 stimulus package funding for struggling small businesses by the Obama administration. While African Americans own 5 percent of the small businesses in the country, they received only 1 percent of the funding from the stimulus package. In comparison, whites received a whopping 92 percent of stimulus package funding even though they only own 82 percent of small businesses. "Overall, white-owned businesses received over $130 million in loans through the program, while Hispanic-owned businesses got $4 million and black-owned businesses [received] less than $2 million" (Glantz, online). With no-interest loans, no payments for 12 months, and five years to pay, stimulus package funding was nothing short of social welfare. It provided a lesser version of "too big to fail" with "too small to fail" for many white American small businesses. Major media reporting on disparities in stimulus funding was nonexistent. This inequitable disbursement of federal bailout funding, like the disparities in business lending practices, has compound effects that place many minority groups at a gross disadvantage. As Javier Palomarez, the president and chief executive officer of the United States Hispanic Chamber of Commerce, explains, "African American and Hispanic entrepreneurs often self-financed their start-ups or expansions, meaning that they tapped into their own net worth taking out home equity loans or second mortgages to invest in their communities and create jobs" (Glantz, online). Such a predicament results in greater fiscal vulnerability for African American and Hispanic small businesses, increasing their likelihood of folding early in the process of national recession, local downward economic spirals, or personal financial struggles.

In a rash of negative publicity highlighting scandalous and even criminal behavior by a small group of highly visible members of the CBC, Representative Waters was charged by the House Ethics Committee with failing to disclose to federal bank regulators her husband's stock holdings in OneUnited Bank and his former board member status. OneUnited Bank received stimulus funding to the tune of $12 million from the government's Troubled Asset Relief Program crafted by the Obama administration. Waters contended that she arranged a meeting with U.S. Treasury officials, not on behalf of OneUnited Bank but for the purpose of bailing out minority banks on behalf of the National Bankers Associate, which represents some 130 minority-owned banks (Waters, online). Waters maintained that she "fully disclosed her assets as required by House rules" and that the Office of Congressional Ethics has "drawn negative inferences where there are none and twisted facts to fit its faulty conclusions" (Waters, online).

In a rather suspicious turn of events following the 2010 midterm elections, the proceedings against Waters were temporarily postponed by the House Ethics Committee because of the questionable conduct of two ethics committee attorneys who were later suspended by the Democratic chairman, Zoe Lofgren of California. Responding to the suspicious postponement of her investigation, Waters blasted, "From the beginning, I have been concerned with the Committee's unsupported conclusions, often contradictory arguments and unfounded native inferences" (Condon, "House Reps," online). It is telling that this controversy received wide media attention even as the inequitable distribution of stimulus funding—which was the real injustice and for which Waters was never credited with exposing—barely registered as newsworthy. While no hard evidence exists that the House Ethics Committee, composed equally of Democrats and Republicans and chaired at the time by a Democrat, manipulated the process to keep Waters and embattled congressman Charles B. Rangel in the media spotlight, the timing of events put a black face on government malfeasance and mismanagement of tax-payers' dollars, which emerged as *the* hot button issue of the midterm elections. As fortuitous as this political blame game was for Republicans, who were riding the wave of the racially charged Tea Party movement, it was also fortuitous for white Democrats on the ballot who wanted to distinguish their political integrity from others within their party.

What all this public rancor within and beyond the Tea Party move-ment over fiscal responsibility covered over, of course, was the fact those at the top of the economic food chain—the overwhelming major-ity of whom are white—did not cotton to the idea of the redistribution of wealth. How else can one explain why the Republican Party and the more radically conservative, Tea Partiers, whose political battle cry was "cut wasteful government spending" and "lower the deficit," made ex-tending Bush-era tax cuts for the wealthy their top priority on entering office. While on the campaign trail Obama stressed that ending these tax cuts would be one of his top priorities as president, he barely put up a fight to stop the measure from moving forward. Forecasting what we could expect from him as he faced a Republican-led Congress, Obama enlisted none other than Bill Clinton to help sell his tax compromise, especially to disenchanted Democrats who viewed the deal with Repub-licans as a breach of trust. Thomas J. Sugrue reminds us that in the late 1990s Obama used to be a vocal skeptic of Clinton's bipartisan initiatives, describing them as bad deals for blacks and the poor. In a 1996 interview in a University of Chicago newspaper Obama argued, "On the national level, bipartisanship usually means Democrats ignore the needs of the poor and abandon the idea that government can play a role in issues of poverty, race discrimination, sex discrimination or environmental protection" (Sugrue, 84). As Obama's star began to rise in politics, how-ever, he switched gears, becoming increasingly more conservative and "adopt[ing] his own version of Clintonian triangulation, offering quali-fied support for affirmative action and endorsing welfare reform, while advocating for the expansion of job training and child care programs, transportation subsidies to smooth the welfare-to-work transition, and the EITC [Earned Income Tax Credit]" (85). In *Audacity of Hope,* Obama states flatly that Bill Clinton and conservatives "were right about welfare as it was previously structured" (303). Suffice it to say, then, Obama's compromise with the Tea Party–charged Republican Party was in line with his conservative, Clintonian political trajectory.

The bill that Obama crafted with Republicans and signed into law on December 2010 cost a whopping $858 billion. Experts predict that measures proposed in the bill will probably boost economic growth but add to the nation's $1.3 trillion budget deficit and may further unsettle the bond market. As part of the bill, the estate tax giveaway puts the top rate at 35 percent after an exemption of $5 million per person. The measure extended unemployment benefits for 13 months for those who qualify and reduced payroll taxes by two percentage points during 2011. As a whole, the bill provided greater spending than the 2008 stimulus package, yet there was no outcry from fiscal hawks or condemnation from Tea Party members. In many respects, this bill flies in the face of fiscal responsibility. Indeed, if the nation is genuinely interested in reducing the ballooning national debt and paying for two simultaneous wars, this was certainly not the answer.

Racial common sense thinking clarifies the contradiction in the 2010 tax cut package between fiscal austerity/deficit reduction and the expressed urgency of the GOP to cut the taxes of the wealthiest Americans. As Shapiro explains, "Middle-class families now are passing along about $9 trillion to their adult children. How they use this unprecedented wealth transfer is an important part of this increasing inequality and racial inequality stories" (42). The swelling American debt has become a threat to the maintenance of the unequivocal wealth disparity that White America has accumulated since its conception—only elite whites have the money to get the country out of its economic woes, and they know it. Thus, the Obama administration received a tremendous amount of backlash in its attempt to deny a continuation of the Bush tax cuts. With the elite, white Tea Partiers helping to steer the economic debate, the idea that the rich should help pay down the debt through taxation was dead on arrival. Sensing the shifting political winds, Obama ripped a page out the Clinton bipartisan compromise book and sold the plan as a necessary evil to ensure that the middle class would continue to receive tax cuts and get extended unemployment benefits. What this compromise ultimately means is that the wealth gap will widen during Obama's presidency and his policies will help to expand it. At the same time, Obama will reside as president during the continuation of a new system of social control ushered in by the War on Drugs, mandatory sentencing guidelines, expanding economic inequality, and self-help as the paramount answer to social welfare for the poor. The urban black poor will bear the brunt of this assault while claims of a post-racial America will drive the political discourse.

Perhaps more troubling than what lies ahead for the urban black poor under Obama's watch is the fact that African Americans, in particular, are the most optimistic group in America when it comes to their social and economic outlook. What should give us all pause is that this wellspring of black optimism—like the (irrational) optimism experienced during the Clinton presidency—is radically out of line with socioeconomic realities. According to analysts who study black prosperity, this (uncritical) optimism is, at once, "rooted in long experience with hard times" and a belief that African American concerns are being attended to at the highest levels of government. In other words, African Americans treat the symbolic capital of having an African American president as if it is as good as gold. It's not even that blacks have set the bar of expectations low for Barack Obama. They don't seem to have set any expectations at all, except that he continue to be articulate, look dignified, and "represent" for the "block." It appears as if the feat of winning the presidency and making history was the end game. If Bill Clinton's presidency is any indication of what African Americans can expect from Barack Obama in the future, this cultural love affair with him may cost us dearly down the road.

## CONCLUSION

> Obama is a professional politician first and last. For the sake of attaining and retaining power, he is willing to adopt, jettison, or manipulate positions as evolving circumstances require. Supporters call it adaptability, detractors opportunism. He has liberal instincts and will effectuate progressive reforms —but only if he can do so without getting uncomfortably close to what he perceives to be too high a political price. That is why progressives need to put grassroots movements on the ground to serve as blockers. If they clear space for Obama on the left he will follow. But he will not himself lead the way.
>
> —Randall Kennedy, *The Persistence of the Colorline*

In an interview with *Democracy NOW!* actor, activist, and civil rights icon, Harry Belafonte was asked to give his assessment of Obama's performance. Not one to mince his words, Belafonte expressed disappointment, saying that he thought Obama had done little, if anything, to attend to the needs of the downtrodden and voiceless communities in the United States. He was even more critical, however, of the American people and black folks in particular for what he viewed as giving Obama a free pass politically by not putting pressure on him to fulfill many of his campaign promises. Belafonte contextualizes his argument with a story that Eleanor Roosevelt shared with him about a meeting her husband, President Franklin D. Roosevelt, had with black union and civil rights activist A. Phillip Randolph. Seizing the moment, Randolph admonished FDR for not doing enough to ensure the civil rights and economic equality of African Americans workers. FDR agreed with Randolph's assessment of his handling of civil rights and then issued a charge to Randolph: "I'd like to ask you to go out and make me do what you think it is I should do. Go out and make me do it" (Goodman, online). Given the racial tensions that existed at that time, Roosevelt was reluctant to speak out about civil rights because of the political hit he would take in the press and among his white constituency. From Roosevelt's vantage point, speaking out in favor of civil rights without political pressure from the outside was far too risky. If, however, he were pressed into reacting by, say, an organized march or sustained political agitation, he would be in a much better position to concede ground and address blacks' civil rights concern. Relating this story back to Barack Obama, Belafonte asserts:

> What is sad for this moment is that there is no force, no energy, of popular voice, popular rebellion, popular upheaval, no champion for radical thought at the table of the discourse. And as a consequence, Barack Obama has nothing to listen to, except his detractors and those who help pave the way to his own personal comfort with power—power contained, power misdirected, power not fully engaged. And it is our task to no longer have expectations of him, unless we have forced him to the table and he still resists us. And if he does that, then we know what else we have to do, is to make change completely. But I think he plays the game that he plays because he sees no threat from evidencing concerns for the poor. He sees no threat from evidencing a deeper concern for the needs of black people, as such. He feels no great threat from evidencing a greater policy towards the international community, for expressing thoughts

that criticize the American position on things and turns that around. Until we
do that, I think we'll be forever disappointed in what that administration will
deliver. (Goodman, online)

Belafonte's keen insights are instructive as it concerns Obama and
the path forward for Black America. He makes clear that we cannot
expect Obama or any politician—regardless of racial background—
to act in good faith. To invoke one of the popular slogans of Obama's
campaign, "We are the change that we have been waiting for." Indeed,
the only way for us to ensure Obama lives up to his campaign pledges,
especially as it regards the urban black poor, is to get off the sidelines
and make our voices heard. The widespread enthusiasm for the Obama
presidential run was nothing short of inspirational. Folks that had never
voted in their lives or even been interested in politics at all became politically engaged. Money poured into his campaign from people who
had never given a dime of their money to a politician. Young people—
who typically do not become excited about politics—were knocking
on doors and canvassing neighborhoods to get out the vote. Even hip
hop artists—unusual suspects in the political spectrum—stepped up
to the plate, putting on fundraisers and even developing theme songs
for the campaign. If we learned anything from this historical moment, it
was that people power really is transformative. The problem, especially
among African Americans, was that after the election we packed up our
tents, pulled up our yard signs, hung up our phones, and assumed that
the "mission" had been accomplished. Obama's conspicuous inattention
to the CBC and Black America at large underscores the problem of this
"mission-accomplished" mindset—a problem, we are sad to say, that
Black America in particular has yet to fully register. Though optimism
in times of trouble is typically a good thing, Black America's uncritical exuberance toward Barack Obama borders on cognitive dissonance.
When Belafonte was asked in this same interview if he was concerned
that his criticism of Obama would undermine Obama's reelection bid, he
responded, "I think we will not only undermine him, but undermine the
hopes of this nation, if we don't criticize him. I believe that patriotism
is betrayed by those voices that are not heard. Those who would detract
you from that fact are those who have a vested interest in maintaining

the status quo" (Goodman, online). It is high time, then, that we stop protecting Obama and start demanding of him what we demand of ourselves. To riff on Derrick Bell's iconic book, *And We Are Not Saved: The Elusive Quest for Racial Justice,* Obama will not save Black America. The more pressing issue is, are we prepared and willing to save ourselves?

# NOTES

INTRODUCTION

1. See, for example, Dowd's op-ed article in the *New York Times*, "Dark Dark Dark," February 21, 2009.

2. In Michigan and New York the African American unemployment rate is now hovering near 30 percent.

3. The other photo juxtaposed to Graythen's in the controversial news story was taken by Dave Martin, a white photographer for the Associated Press.

4. Lt. Gen. Russel Honore's actions also earned him instant folk hero status in black communities.

1. THE TEACHING MOMENT THAT NEVER WAS

1. It has often been the case historically that when blacks held a class status advantage over their white peers in such confrontations, it wasn't necessarily an advantage for the blacks. "Uppity negroes/niggers," as whites typically tagged such wealthy or outspoken and articulate black folks, represented an even greater perceived threat to the white status quo than the black working-class and poor masses.

2. Indeed, Gates's primary claim to fame as an academician is not necessarily scholastic. That he has made important and lasting intellectual contributions to the discourse cannot be denied. However, his celebrity within black intellectual communities and in the public domain is due in large measure to how he helped "innovate" and brand African American studies in higher education. As Harris-Perry explains, "Gates used the inherent competitiveness of Ivy League institutions to create a hyperelite niche for the very best black academics. His strategy improved the market value of black intellectuals throughout the academy and the public sphere" ("Skip Gates," online).

3. Gates has long championed an anti-essentialist approach to black identity, a mindset that is largely compatible with post-racialist thinking.

4. When the story of Gates's arrest first broke, famed African American satirist and provocateur Ishmael Reed penned a rather contentious essay that blasted Gates's postracial mindset and characterized his arrest as a kind of poetic justice.

5. The Birthers are a conservative, fringe group that believes—despite substantiated evidence to the contrary—that Barack Obama is not a natural-born citizen and thus is not legally qualified to be president of the United States.

6. The Tea Party Patriots is an organization composed largely of disaffected Republicans who want conservatives to return to the core principles of the party under Ronald Reagan. They famously depicted President Obama as an African witch doctor during a televised protest against his health care initiative.

7. Important to note is that the Joe Wilson issue would have probably been squashed —at least in Congress—had it not been for House Majority Whip James Clyburn of South Carolina. An African American and staunch civil rights activist, Clyburn led the charge to censure Joe Wilson before Congress, explaining, "My father used to say, 'Son, always remember that silence gives consent'" (Kleefield, online).

## 2. "I KNOW WHAT'S IN HIS HEART"

1. In his essay "10 Myths about Legacy Preferences in College Admissions," Richard D. Kahlenberg explains that legacy admissions were established following World War I "as a reaction to an influx of immigrant students, particularly Jews, into America's selective colleges" (online).

2. See James Weldon Johnson's *The Autobiography of an Ex-Coloured Man* and James Baldwin's *The Fire Next Time.*

3. See Barbara Christian's iconic essay, "A Race for Theory."

4. In his essay, "What America Would Be Like without Blacks" in *Going to the Territory,* Ellison writes, "Many whites could look at the social position of blacks and feel that color formed an easy and reliable gauge for determining to what extent one was or was not American. . . . But this is *tricky magic.* Despite his racial difference and social status, something indisputably American about Negroes not only raised doubts about the white man's value system but aroused the troubling suspicion that whatever else the true American is, he is also somehow black" (my emphasis, 111).

5. Ferraro's stated, "If Obama was a white man, he would not be in this position. And if he was a woman of any color, he would not be in this position. He happens to be very lucky to be who he is. And the country is caught up in the concept" ("Clinton-Backer Ferraro," online).

6. Steele, who is also biracial, often projects his experiences as a mixed-raced man struggling with racial identity and masculinity onto Obama.

7. The white farmer, who consequently shot Sherrod's father (Hosie Miller) in the back, was acquitted of wrongdoing by an all-white jury.

## 3. THE AUDACITY OF REVEREND WRIGHT

1. This critique occurs before Malcolm X's split with the Nation of Islam and its blackcentric doctrine.

2. When discussing the various ways in which African American children in the United States learn versus their white Eurocentric peers, Wright operates from a static notion of African tradition that collapses the immense diversity of African cultures. In doing so, he plays up a problematic and overdetermined idea of a fluid and conflict-free diasporic African identity. Thus, he winds up reinforcing a version of the myopic white supremacist racial thinking that he is consciously trying to dismantle in his speech.

3. Sam Hose was a "literate" laborer who was brutally and ritualistically lynched in 1899 by a white mob after he killed a white man (who refused to pay a debt) in self-defense. The media and politicians recast the self-defense act as premeditated murder and accused Hose of raping the white man's wife—an accusation that even the white man's wife vehemently denied.

4. See Hendrick's essay "A More Perfect (High-Tech) Lynching: Obama, the Press, and Jeremiah Wright."

5. Addressing the issue in a *New York Times* op-ed article, "After Attacks, Michelle Obama Looks for a New Introduction," reporters Michael Powell and Jodi Kantor relayed, "Obama stopped that [experiment]. The prospect of white doctors performing a trial with black teenage girls summoned [for Michelle Obama] the specter of the Tuskegee syphilis experiment of the mid-20th century."

6. See Gwen Ifill's discussion of Obama's courting of the white elite in *The Breakthrough: Politics and the Race in the Age of Obama*.

7. See Walton's *Watch This: The Ethics and Aesthetics of Black Televangelism*.

8. See Jackson's essay, "Wright Stuff, Wrong Time, Part 1," in *The Speech: Race and the Barack Obama's "A More Perfect Union."*

## 4. SETTING THE RECORD STRAIGHT

1. Smiley has been very open about what he viewed as a snub by then-presidential candidate Barack Obama in failing to attend Smiley's annual State of the Black Union forum in 2008 (Obama offered to send his wife Michelle in his absence). Smiley has taken heat, particularly within black spaces, because of his tendency to reference this "snub" in the media when expressing his frustration with President Obama's inattentiveness toward black poverty and a lack of a black agenda (West has also been vocal about the fact that Obama did not send him an invitation to the inauguration despite his vigorous campaigning on Obama's behalf). The venom in the black media was particularly intense during Smiley and West's 2011 "poverty tour." Both Tom Joyner and Steve Harvey took swipes at the poverty tour for what they perceived as a publicity stunt driven by individual pettiness rather than an altruistic political impulse. Though West was roundly lampooned as well, Smiley was singled out as being particularly petty.

2. On February 2011 the *Washington Post* reported that despite the fact that "African-Americans and Hispanics were more likely to be left broke, jobless and concerned that they lack the skills needed to shape their economic futures" they somehow "remained the most hopeful that the economy would soon right itself and allow them to prosper." In stark contrast, whites, who fared better financially during the recession than African Americans and Hispanics, "are the most resentful of government action and far less optimistic about what is ahead financially, both for their own families and for the country as whole" (Cohen and Fletcher, online).

3. Cornel West took fire from Al Sharpton on an MSNBC special addressing the black agenda. When West took Sharpton to task for being a "black mascot" for the Obama administration, Sharpton took offense and launched into a tirade against West and black academics in general for "talking" instead of acting on the ground in the service of Black America.

4. A 2011 PEW Research Center document on the wealth gap among racial and ethnic groups revealed, "The net worth of black households fell from $12,124 in 2005 to $5,677

in 2009, a decline of 53%" (7). This compares to a 66% lost of wealth among Hispanics and a mere 16% household net worth lost for whites during the same period.

## 5. PULL YOURSELF UP BY YOUR BOOTSTRAPS

1. For the record, Morrison has since explained that her comments were taken out of context. She says that her intent was not to bestow Clinton with honorary blackness but simply to highlight the ways in which, during the highly publicized sex scandal during his stint in office, he was treated in the media and the courts like he was culturally black (read: a second-class citizen).

2. We are making a distinction here between elite and wealthy white planters and the white masses, many of whom were indentured servants and treated little better than enslaved Africans before laws were created in the colonies to outlaw such treatment of poor whites.

3. It was common practice during slavery for whites to encourage enslaved Africans to betray each other. The FBI also used similar tactics of encouraging betrayal and, in many instances, planting spies during the Civil Rights/Black Power Movements to try to dismantle key organizations.

4. Throughout the majority of blacks' history in the United States, challenging white authority—even symbolically—has been met with white violence and, in many cases, even death.

5. Winant argues that traditional civil rights legislation moderated "the problems of racial injustice and inequality . . . but hardly resolved" them. The "colorblind" approach to addressing racial injustice and inequality that grew out of this legislation reinforced the idea that we should eliminate race as a factor in evaluating individuals in all facets of society. Though such thinking is premised on faulty logic and covers over the striking advantages of white privilege and institutionalized white supremacy, it has become the new racial common sense of the twenty-first century. "As a result, the already limited racial reform policies (affirmative action, etc.) and the relatively powerless state agencies charged with enforcing civil rights laws (EEOC) developed in the 1960s have undergone several decades of severe attack. Forceful arguments have been made that the demands of the civil rights movement have largely been met, and that the United States has entered a 'postracial' stage of its history. Advocates of this position—usually classified as 'neoconservatives' but sometimes also found on the left—have ceaselessly instructed racially defined minorities to 'pull themselves up by their own bootstraps' and in callous distortion of Martin Luther King Jr.'s message, have exhorted them to accept the 'content of their character' (rather than 'the color of their skin') as the basic social value of the country" (115).

6. Tom Joyner quipped that he was "jumped on" by many African Americans when he blamed both gubernatorial losses on Obama's inattentiveness to black concerns: "All I said was the president needs to talk to his black base . . . [these gubernatorial loses are] an indication that if you don't address [black concerns] . . . we don't go to the polls" ("The Tom Joyner Morning Show," online).

7. The tricky balance with addressing black concerns for Obama is exacerbated by the rise of white minority politics as a backlash to shifting demographic trends that predict whites will no longer be the dominant group in terms of population and political power. In *Wingnuts: How the Lunatic Fringe Is Hijacking America*, John Alvon asserts that there is a fear among a white conservative minority that the traditional national heritage may

be eclipsed by midcentury due to the rising numbers of a non-white majority. For this fringe group, then, the election of a black man to the presidency is cause for panic. As Alvon opines, "The presence of the first African American president is driving another anxiety—the change from a traditionally white to minority-led federal government" (4).

8. After making extraordinary gains in math and reading proficiency in the 1970s and 1980s, African American public school children and youth still remain considerably behind their white counterparts in academic achievement. Nearly 45% of public school students who drop out are African Americans and only 50% of Black youth graduate from high school. Moreover, given that we are now more than 50 years past *Brown vs. Board of Education*, only 46% of African American children attend high schools where graduation is the norm. Comparatively, over 95% of white students attend high schools where graduation is the norm (Brown, et al.,105).

9. The Bradley Effect is the theory that in a political race involving a white and non-white, whites will tell pollsters that they are either undecided or voting for the non-white candidate only to vote for the white candidate on election day. It was named after Los Angeles mayor Tom Bradley, an African American, who lost a bid for California's governor race in 1982 to a white candidate George Deukmejian even though the polls leading up to the race showed he had a comfortable lead.

10. Obama later granted their request for a meeting.

# WORKS CITED

*The Al Sharpton Show.* Interview with Charles Olgetree and Tavis Smiley. Feb. 23, 2010.

Avlon, John. *Wingnuts: How the Lunatic Fringe Is Hijacking America* Philadelphia: Beast Books, 2010. Print.

Baker, Houston A., Jr. *Betrayal: How Black Intellectuals Have Abandoned the Ideals of the Civil Rights Era.* New York: Columbia UP, 2008.

Baldwin, James. *The Cross of Redemption Uncollected Writing.* New York: Pantheon Books. 2009. Print.

———. *The Fire Next Time.* New York: Vintage, 1962. Print.

———. *Nobody Knows My Name.* New York: New York Dial Press, 1961.

Balz, Dan. "Biden Stumbles at the Starting Gate." *Washingtonpost.com.* Feb. 1, 2007 (online). June 13, 2010.

Bell, Derrick. *And We Are Not Saved: The Elusive Quest for Racial Justice.* Basic Books, 1987. Print.

———. *Silent Covenants: Brown v. Board of Education and the Unfulfilled Hopes for Racial Reform.* New York: Oxford UP, 2004. Print.

Blitstein, Ryan. "Racism's Hidden Toll." *Miller-McCune* June 15, 2009 (online). Nov. 28, 2009.

Bradford, William D. "The Wealth Dynamics of Entrepreneurship for Black and White Families in the U.S." *Review of Income and Wealth.* March 5, 2003 (online). January 20, 2010.

Brown, Micheal K., et al. *White-Washing Race: The Myth of A Color-Blind Society.* U of California P, 2003. Print.

Campbell, Horace. *Barack Obama and 21st Century Politics: A Revolutionary Moment in the USA.* New York: St. Martin's Press. 2010. Print.

Christian, Barbara. "A Race for Theory." *Cultural Critique.* 6 (Spring 1987): 51–63. Print.

Christie, Ron. *Acting White: The Curious History of a Racial Slur.* St. Martin's Press, 2010. Print.

"Clinton-Backer Ferraro: Obama Where He Is Because He's Black." *ABCnews.com.* March 11, 2008 (online). April 15, 2009.

Cobb, William Jelani. *The Substance of Hope*. New York: Walker Publishing Co, 2010. Print.

Cohen, Jon, and Micheal A. Fletcher. "Poll Finds Minorities More Optimistic about Economy Despite Losses." *Washington Post*. Feb. 20, 2011 (online). May 25, 2011.

Collins, Dan. "Dad Slams Attack on Bush At King Rite." *CBSnews.com*. Feb. 11, 2009. (online). January 5, 2010.

"'Coming After You!': Wright Vows to Hold Obama Accountable If Elected." Breitbart TV.com. April 28, 2008 (online).

Condon, Stephanie. "Gay Rights Activists Protest Obama Fundraiser, Lash Out against White House." cbs *News*. October 12, 2010 (online). April 4, 2011.

———. "House Raps Rep. Maxine Waters on Ethics Charge." cbs *News*. August 2, 2010 (online). Feb. 22, 2011.

Cooper, Helene. "Attorney General Chided for Language on Race." *New York Times*, March 8, 2009: A26.

Cooper, Helene, and Abby Goodnough. "Over Beers, No Apologies, but Plans to Have Lunch." *New York Times*, July 31, 2009 (online). July 31, 2009.

Dead Prez. "Politrickkks." Single. Dead Prez Inc., 2008.

"Democratic Presidential Debate." hosted by cnn. YouTube. 21 Jan. 2008. Web. 24 May 2011.

DeNava-Walt, Carmen, Bernadette D. Proctor, and Jessica C. Smith. U.S. Census Bureau, *Current Population Reports, P60–238, Income, Poverty, and Health Insurance Coverage in the United States: 2009*. Washington, DC: U.S. Government Printing Office.

Dowd, Maureen. "Boy, Oh, Boy." *nytimes.com*. 12 Sept. 2009 (online). Sept 29, 2009.

Drash, Wayne. "911 caller in Gates arrest never referred to 'black suspects.'" *CNN.com* 27 July, 2009 (online). July 27, 2009.

Du Bois, W. E. B. *The Souls of Black Folk*. New York: Pocket Books, 2005.

Dyson, Marcia. "Take Me to the Waters." *Huff Post Black Voices*. 28 Sept 2011 (online.) Sept 10, 2011.

Dyson, Michael Eric. *Is Bill Cosby Right?: Or Has the Black Middle Class Lost Its Mind?* New York: Basic Civitas Books, 2005.

Edney, Hazel. T. "cbc Demands Fair Share for African Americans." *Tri-State Defender*. Dec. 17, 2009 (online). Oct. 13, 2010.

Ehrenreich, Barbara, and Dedrick Muhammed. "The Destruction of the Black Middle Class." *Huffington Post*. 4 Aug. 2009 (online). Sept. 11, 2009.

Ellison, Ralph. *Going to the Territory*. New York: Random House, 1986.

———. "Harlem Is Nowhere." In *Shadow and Act*. New York: Random House, 1953.

———. "The World and the Jug." In *Shadow and Act*. New York: Random House, 1953.

Farhi, Paul. "Tavis Smiley Will Cut Ties with Joyner Radio Show." *Washington Post*. April 12, 2008 (online). August 19, 2010.

Faulkner, William. *Requiem for a Nun*. New York: Random House, 1951.

Fauntroy, Michael. *A Black Agenda for President Obama to Address? Yes!* Huffingtonpost.com. Feb. 4, 2010 (online). March 17, 2011.

Fry, Richard, et al. "Wealth Gaps Rise to Record Highs Between White, Blacks and Hispanics," Pew Social & Demographic Trends. July 26, 2011 (online). August 27, 2011.

Gans, Herbert J. "The Uses of Poverty: The Poor Pay All." *Social Policy.* July/August (1971): 20–24. Print.

Glantz, Aaron. "Minority Businesses Shut Out of Stimulus Loans." *New American Media.* Dec. 17, 2009 (online). Feb. 8, 2010.

Goldman, David. "Black Unemployment 'a Serious Problem.'" CNN *Money* Dec. 4, 2009 (online). May 10, 2009.

Goodman, Amy. *Harry Belafonte on Obama:* "He Plays the Game That He Plays Because He Sees No Threat from Evidencing Concerns for the Poor." *Democracy Now.* Jan. 26, 2011 (online). Jan 27, 2011.

Grossman, Harvey. "Illinois Must Act on Racial Profiling." ACLU. Aug. 3, 2009 (online). Sept. 5, 2009.

Guinier, Lani. "Race and Reality in a Front-Porch Encounter." *Chronicle of Higher Education,* July 30, 2009. July 30, 2009.

Halperin, Mark, and John Heilemann. *Game Change.* New York: Harper Collins, 2010. Print.

Harris, Hamil R. "Lowery Defends His Criticism of Bush at Coretta King Funeral." *Washington Post.* Feb. 22, 2006 (online). June 10, 2010.

Harris-Lacewell, Melissa. "The Clinton Fallacy: Did Blacks Really Make Big Economic Gains during the '90s?" *Slate.* Jan. 24, 2008 (online). June 8, 2011.

———. "Skip Gates and the Post-Racial Project." *Nation,* July 21, 2009 (online). July 22, 2009.

Henderson, David R. "Jeremiah Wright: True and False." *Antiwar.com,* March 20, 2008. (online) Feb. 15, 2011.

Hendricks, Obery M., Jr., "A More Perfect (High-Tech) Lynching: Obama, the Press, and Jeremiah Wright." *The Speech: Race and Barack Obama's "A More Perfect Union."* Ed. T. Denean Sharpley-Whiting. New York: Bloomsbury, 2009. 155–183.

"Henry Louis Gates, Jr. Police Report." *Smoking Gun.* July 23, 2009. Sept. 15, 2009.

Herbert, Bob. "Anger Has Its Place." *New York Times,* Aug. 1, 2009 (online). Sept. 5, 2009.

Holland, Steve. "Senate's Reid Tells Obama He Regrets Racial Remarks." *Reuters,* Jan. 10, 2010 (online). May 15, 2010.

Hutchinson, E. O. "Hang in There Tavis Smiley, Don't Let the Black Obama Thought Police Run You Out." *Huffington Post,* April 11, 2008 (online). March 13, 2010.

"I Quit." *bet.com/news,* April 14, 2008 (online). March 17, 2010.

Ifill, Gwen. *The Breakthrough: Politics and the Race in the Age of Obama.* New York: Random House, 2009. Print.

*An Inconvenient Truth.* Dir. Davis Guggenheim. Perf. Al Gore and Billy West (II). Paramount, 2006.

Jackson, David. "Obama Rejects Congressional Black Caucus Criticism." USA *Today.* 3 Dec 2009. Web. 12 April 2011.

Jackson, John. *Racial Paranoia.* New York, Basic Civitas, 2008.

Jacobs, Harriet. *Incidents in the Life of a Slave Girl.* Eds. Frances Smith Foster and Nellie Y. McKay. New York: W.W. Norton, 2001. First published 1861. Print.

"Jesse Jr: Obama's 'Political Future' Not My Top Concern." Politico.com. March 5, 2010 (online). June 20, 2011.

Jhally, Sut, and Justin Lewis. "White Responses: The Emergence of 'Enlightened' Racism." *Channeling Blackness: Studies on Television and Race in America.* Ed. Darnell M. Hunt. Oxford UP, 2004. 74–88. Print.

Johnson, James Weldon. *The Autobiography of an Ex-Colored Man.* Dover Publications, 1995. Print.

Kahlenberg, Richard D. "10 Myths about Legacy Preferences in College Admissions." *Chronicle of Higher Education.* Sept. 22, 2010 (online). Oct 15, 2010.

Kelley, Robin. D. G. *Yo' Mama's Disfunktional!: Fighting the Culture Wars in Urban America.* Boston: Beacon Press. 1997. Print.

Kennedy, Randall. *The Persistence of the Colorline: Racial Politics and the Obama Presidency.* New York: Pantheon Books. 2011. Print.

King, Martin Luther, Jr. "Beyond Vietnam—A Time to Break the Silence." *American Rhetoric. Online Speech Bank.* (online) May 15, 2011.

———. "Letter from a Birmingham Jail." *The Norton Anthology of African American Literature.* Ed. Henry Louis Gates Jr. and Nellie Y. McKay. New York: Norton, 2004. 1895–1896. Print.

Kinney, Aaron. "'Looting' or 'Fnding.'" *Salon,* Sep. 1, 2005 (online). Oct. 5, 2009.

Kleefeld, Eric. "Clyburn Emerges as Lead Dem against Joe Wilson." *TPMDC,* 15 Sept. 2009 (online). Sept. 15, 2009.

Long, David A., and Tammy Ouellette. "Private Employers and TANF Recipients," U.S. Department of Labor, 2004.

Lowery, Joseph, Rev. "Comments at Coretta Scott King's Funeral." YouTube, Feb. 7, 2006 (online) 19 Sept. 2010.

Lerer, Lisa, and Nia-Malika Henderson. "Congressional Black Caucus: President Obama's Not Listening." *Politico.* March 11, 2010 (online). March 13, 2011.

Mansbach, Adam. "The Audacity of Post-Racism." *The Speech: Race and Barack Obama's 'A More Perfect Union.'"* Ed. T. Denean Sharpley-Whiting. New York: Bloomsbury, 2009. 69–84. Print.

Marable, Manning. *How Capitalism Underdeveloped Black America: Problems in Race, Political Economy, and Society.* Cambridge, UK: South End Press, 2000. Print.

McWhorter, John. "Gates Is Right—and We're Not Post-Racial Until He's Wrong." *New Republic* July 22, 2009 (online). Sept. 4, 2009.

Miah, Malik. "Race & Class: Obama & the Politics of Protest." *IV Online Magazine,* May 24, 2010 (online). June 24, 2011.

"Michelle Obama: 'For the First Time in My Adult Lifetime, I'm Really Proud of My Country.'" *ABC News.* Feb. 18, 2008 (online). March 23, 2010.

Miga, Andrew. "Barney Frank: Gay Rights March 'A Waste of Time At Best.'" *Huffington Post,* Oct. 10, 2009 (online). 17 March 2010.

Montopoll, Brian. "Unpacking Harry Reid's 'Racist' Comments." *CBS News,* Jan. 11, 2010 (online). May 15, 2010.

Moyers, Bill. "Bill Moyers Interviews Rev. Jeremiah Wright." *Bill Moyers Journal,* April 24, 2008 (online). July 10, 2010.

Muhammad, Dedrick. "Race and Extreme Inequality." *Nation,* June 30, 2008. Print.

Myers, S. L. "Presidential address—Analysis of race and policy analysis." *Journal of Policy Analysis and Management."* 21.2 (2002): 169–190. Print.

No Child Left Behind Act. Education of 2001. Intergovernmental relations 20 U.S.C. 6301 (2001).

Noguera, Pedro. "Reframing the Schools Debate." *Nation*. Dec. 20, 2010. Print.

Obama, Barack. *Audacity of Hope*. New York: Three Rivers Press, 2006. Print.

Obama, Barack. *The Audacity of Hope: Thoughts on Reclaiming the American Dream*. New York: Random House. 2006.

"Obama's Ratings Slide Across the Board: The Economy, Health Care Reform and Gates Grease the Skids." Pew Research Center for the People and the Press. July 30, 2009 (online). July 30, 2009.

Office of Policy Planning and Research, U.S. Department of Labor. *The Negro Family: The Case For National Action*. Dol.gov. March 1965 (online).

Olopade, Dayo. "Skip Gates Speaks." *The Root*, July 21, 2009 (online). Aug. 5, 2009.

Oinounou, Moshuh, and Bonney Kapp. "Michelle Obama Takes Heat for Saying She's Proud of Country for First Time." *Fox News*, Feb. 19, 2008 (online). Nov. 10, 2009.

Neal, Mark Anthony. "Rage of the Thinking Class." Seeingblack.com, July 22, 2009 (online). July 22, 2009.

Powell, John. A. *Race, Place, and Opportunity*. The Color of Opportunity. *American Prospect. Special Report*. October 2008. Print.

Powell, Michael, and Jodi Kantor. "After Attacks, Michelle Obama Looks for a New Introduction." *New York Times*. June 18, 2008: A1. Print.

Prashad, Vijay. *Everybody Was Kung Fu Fighting: Afro-Asian Connections and the Myth of Cultural Purity*. Boston: Beacon Press, 2001. Print.

Ravitch, Diane. *The Death and Life of the Great American School System: How Testing and Choice Are Undermining Education*. Philadelphia: Basic Books, 2010. Print.

———. "In Need of a Renaissance: Real Reform Will Renew, Not Abandon, Our Neighborhood Schools." *American Educator*. Summer (2010): 10–22. Print.

Reed, Ishmael. "How Henry Louis Gates Got Ordained as the Nation's 'Leading Black Intellectual': Post-Race Scholar Yells Racism." *Counterpunch* July 27, 2009 (online). July 27, 2009.

"Rev. Joseph Lowery Defends His Remarks at the King Funeral." *Hannity and Colmes. Fox News*. Feb. 9, 2006 (online). May 15, 2010.

Richardson, Michael. "FBI Agents That Spied on Martin Luther King Also Ran COINTELPRO Operation Against 'Omaha Two.'" OpEdNews.com. January 2009 (online). Aug. 1, 2010.

Ryan, April. "Interview with President Barack Obama." *Huffington Post*. Dec. 21, 2009 (online). Nov. 7, 2010.

Santayana, George. *Reason in Common Sense, Vol. 1 "of Life Reason."* 1905. New York: Dover Publications, 1980. Print.

Sargent, Greg. "Obama Defends Biden after Moderator Smacks Him on Race." TPM. Dec. 13, 2010 (online). June 28, 2010.

Savage, Barbara Dianne. *Your Spirits Walk Beside Us*. Cambridge: Harvard UP, 2008. Print.

Shakur, Tupac. "Changes." Greatest Hits. Interscope Records, 1998.

Shapiro, Thomas M.. *The Hidden Cost of Being African American: How Wealth Perpetuates Inequality*. New York: Oxford UP, 2004. Print.

Shierholz, Heidi and Edwards, Kathryn. "Jobs Report Offers No Sign of Light at End of Tunnel." Economic Policy Institute. April 3, 2009 (online). April 19, 2010.

Smiley, Tavis, and Stephanie Robinson. *Accountable: Making America as Good as Its Promise*. New York: The Smiley Group, 2009. Print.

Steele, Shelby. *A Bound Man: Why We Are Excited about Obama and Why He Can't Win*. New York: Free Press, 2008. Print.

Stoesz, David. *Quixote's Ghost: The Right, the Liberati, and the Future of Social Policy*. New York: Oxford UP, 2005. Print.

Stolberg, Sheryl G. "For Obama, Nuance on Race Invites Questions." *New York Times*. Feb. 9, 2010 (online). March 17, 2010.

Sue, Derald Wing. *Microaggressions in Everyday Life: Race, Gender, and Sexual Orientation*. Hoboken, NJ: John Wiley, 2010. Print.

Sugrue, Thomas J. *Not Even Past: Barack Obama and the Burden of Race*. Princeton, NJ: Princeton UP, 2010. Print.

Sweet, Lynn. "Obama Tells Lynn Sweet Police Acted 'Stupidly' in Arresting Gates." *Chicago Sun-Times*. July 22, 2009. July 22, 2009.

———. "Obama's NAACP Speech, New York, July 16, 2009. Transcript" *Chicago Sun-Times*. July 16, 2009 (online). July 18, 2009.

"Tavis Smiley Quits Tom Joyner." Maynard Institute. 11 April 2008 (online). Feb. 16, 2011.

Teasley, Martell. "School Social Workers and Urban Education Reform: Realities, Advocacy, and Strategies for Change." *School Community Journal* 14.2 (2004): 19–39. Print.

"The Tom Joyner Morning Show." Tavis Smiley Commentary. Feb. 23, 2010.

"The Tom Joyner Morning Show." *YouTube*. 2009 (online). Nov. 4, 2010.

"Transcript: Rev. Jeremiah Wright Speech to National Press Club." *Chicago Tribune*. April 28, 2008 (online). June 12, 2010.

United States, Dept. of Justice. "Remarks as Prepared for Delivery by Attorney General Eric Holder at the Department of Justice African American History Month Program." Washington: US Dept. of Justice. Feb 18, 2009 (online). Oct. 10, 2009.

United States, Dept. of Labor. Bureau of Labor Statistics. *Employment Situation Summary*. Bureau of Labor Statistics, Nov. 6, 2009 (online). Nov. 10, 2009.

Vedantam, Shankar. *Hidden Brain: How Our Unconscious Minds Elect Presidents, Control Markets, Wage Wars, and Save Our Lives*. New York: Random House, 2010.

———. "Shades of Prejudice." *New York Times*. Jan. 18, 2010 (online). Feb. 12, 2010.

Walker, Clarence E., and Gregory D. Smithers. *The Preacher and the Politician*. Charlottesville: U of Virginia P, 2009. Print.

Walton, Jonathan L. *Watch This!: The Ethics and Aesthetics of Black Televangelism*. New York: NYU Press, 2009. Print.

Waters, Maxine. "Congresswoman Waters Challenges Investigation." Press Release. 2 Aug. 2010. Web. 11 Nov 2011.

Wells, Kathleen. "A Conversation with Dr. Cornel West." *Race-Talk*. Feb. 23, 2010 (online). April 4, 2011.

White, KJ. "Re: Obama 'surprised' by Flap over comments on Police." *USA Today*. July 24, 2009 (online). July 25, 2009.

Winant, Howard. *The New Politics of Race: Globalism, Difference, Justice*. Minneapolis: U of Minnesota P, 2004. Print.

Wise, Tim. *Between Barack and a Hard Place: Racism and White Denial in the Age of Obama*. San Francisco: City Lights Books, 2009.

Wright, David. "The Profiling of Sgt. Crowley: The Reason for Gates's Arrest? His Own Hubris." *Chronicle of Higher Education.* July 30, 2009 (online). Nov. 15, 2009.

Wright, Jeremiah. "Confusing God and Government." Trinity United Church of Christ. Chicago, IL. April 13, 2003. Sermon.

# INDEX

DAVID H. IKARD is Associate Professor of English at Florida State University. He is author of *Breaking the Silence: Toward a Black Male Feminist Criticism,* and his essays have appeared in *African American Review, Palimpsest,* MELUS, CLA, *Journal of Black Studies,* and *Obsidian II Journal.* He has also been awarded a Ford Foundation Postdoctoral Fellowship. His blog, "Nation of Cowards," takes up contemporary racial topics and engages a wider intellectual and activist community.

MARTELL LEE TEASLEY is Professor and Chair of the Department of Social Work at the University of Texas at San Antonio. His articles have appeared in numerous journals, including *Children & School, Journal of Emotional and Behavioral Disorders,* and *Journal of Indigenous Voices in Social Work.*